KIDS CAN COOK
ANYTHING!

AMERICA'S
TEST KITCHEN

OTHER COOKBOOKS FROM AMERICA'S TEST KITCHEN KIDS

The Complete Cookbook for Young Chefs
#1 *New York Times* best seller, 2019 IACP Cookbook Award winner for Children, Youth & Family

The Complete Baby and Toddler Cookbook
2020 IACP Cookbook Award nominee for Children, Youth & Family

The Complete Baking Book for Young Chefs
New York Times best seller, 2020 IACP Cookbook Award winner for Children, Youth & Family

My First Cookbook

The Complete DIY Cookbook for Young Chefs
2021 IACP Cookbook Award nominee for Children, Youth & Family

The Complete Cookbook for Young Scientists

The Complete Cookbook for Teen Chefs

Gaby's Latin American Kitchen by Gaby Melian

PRAISE FOR AMERICA'S TEST KITCHEN KIDS

"The inviting, encouraging tone, which never talks down to the audience; emphasis on introducing and reinforcing basic skills; and approachable, simplified recipes make this a notable standout among cookbooks for kids." —*Booklist*, starred review, on *The Complete Cookbook for Young Chefs*

"A must-have book . . . a great holiday buy, too."
—*School Library Journal*, on *The Complete Cookbook for Young Chefs*

"Inspiring not just a confidence in executing delicious recipes but encouraging them to build foundational kitchen skills." —The Takeout, on *The Complete Cookbook for Young Chefs*

"For kids who are interested in cooking . . . [*The Complete Cookbook for Young Chefs*] introduces kids to all the basics . . . and of course there's a whole lot of easy and very tasty recipes to try." —NPR's *Morning Edition*, on *The Complete Cookbook for Young Chefs*

"Having cooked through several cookbooks from America's Test Kitchen, I have come to expect thoroughness, thoughtfulness, attention to detail and helpful troubleshooting, all of which create delicious results. It comes as no surprise that when ATK decided to create a cookbook for kids, *The Complete Cookbook for Young Chefs*, the same standards applied." —*The Dallas Morning News*, on *The Complete Cookbook for Young Chefs*

"America's Test Kitchen has long been a reliable source of advice for home cooks. The kitchen tests tools, techniques and recipes before making recommendations through its TV show, magazines and cookbooks. Now, all that know-how is becoming accessible to kids in *The Complete Cookbook for Young Chefs*." —NPR, on *The Complete Cookbook for Young Chefs*

"This book makes baking accessible . . . An inclusive and welcoming text for young chefs." —*Booklist*, on *The Complete Baking Book for Young Chefs*

"A must-have book to keep your young adult cookbook section up-to-date and to support the current trend of creative young bakers. A contemporary and educational cookbook that's once again kid-tested and kid-approved." —*School Library Journal*, starred review, on *The Complete Baking Book for Young Chefs*

"The cooks at America's Test Kitchen have done a wonderful job of assembling appetizing and slyly audacious recipes for babies and young children." —*The Wall Street Journal*, on *The Complete Baby and Toddler Cookbook*

"This wonderfully interactive, non-messy introduction to baking, though especially designed for preschoolers, will be an instant hit with readers of all ages." —*School Library Journal*, on *Stir Crack Whisk Bake*

"The story is a fun concept, and Tarkela's realistic digital illustration offers the pleasing details of a television studio." —*Publishers Weekly*, on *Cookies for Santa*

"Many 11-year-olds like to get in the kitchen. With this cookbook, they can make over 70 delicious recipes. The best part, however, is that the cookbook explains why food cooks the way it does, and it includes science experiments they can do in the kitchen." —*Insider*, on *The Complete Cookbook for Young Scientists*

"A comprehensive cookbook designed for and tested by teen cooks . . . The layout is crisp and clear, starting with ingredients and their prep, with required equipment highlighted for easy visibility." —*Kirkus Reviews*, starred review, on *The Complete Cookbook for Teen Chefs*

"Kids will love the colorful site and its plentiful selection of recipes, projects, and cooking lessons." —*USA Today*, on America's Test Kitchen Kids website

Library of Congress Cataloging-in-Publication Data is on file with the publisher.

AMERICA'S TEST KITCHEN
21 Drydock Avenue, Boston, MA 02210

Printed in Canada
9 8 7 6 5 4 3 2 1

Distributed by Penguin Random House
Publisher Services
Tel: 800.733.3000

FRONT COVER
Photography: Kevin White

Food Styling: Catrine Kelty

Editor in Chief: Molly Birnbaum

Executive Food Editor: Suzannah McFerran

Executive Editor: Kristin Sargianis

Deputy Food Editor: Afton Cyrus

Associate Editors: Tess Berger, Katy O'Hara, Andrea Rivera Wawrzyn

Test Cooks: Cassandra Loftlin, Faye Yang

Assistant Test Cook: Kristen Bango

Photo Test Cook: Ashley Stoyanov

Editorial Assistant: Julia Arwine

Design Director: Lindsey Timko Chandler

Deputy Art Director: Janet Taylor

Art Director: Gabi Homonoff

Associate Art Director: Molly Gillespie

Photography Director: Julie Bozzo Cote

Senior Photographer: Daniel J. van Ackere

Photographer: Kevin White

Food Styling: Joy Howard, Catrine Kelty, Chantal Lambeth, Gina McCreadie, Kendra McKnight, Ashley Moore, Christie Morrison, Marie Piraino, Elle Simone Scott, Kendra Smith, Sally Staub

Senior Photo Producer: Meredith Mulcahy

Photo Shoot Kitchen Team:
    Test Kitchen Director: Erin McMurrer
    Manager: Alli Berkey
    Lead Test Cook: Eric Haessler
    Test Cooks: Hannah Fenton, Jacqueline Gochenouer, Gina McCreadie, Christa West
    Assistant Test Cook: Hisham Hassan

Senior Video Producer: KeeHup Yong

Video Producer: Kenzie Gruenig

Assistant Video Editor: Anny Guerzon

Senior Print Production Specialist: Lauren Robbins

Production and Imaging Coordinator: Amanda Yong

Production and Imaging Specialists: Tricia Neumyer, Dennis Noble

Project Manager, Publishing Operations: Katie Kimmerer

Lead Copy Editor: Rachel Schowalter

Copy Editors: Christine Campbell, April Poole, Katrina Munichiello

Chief Creative Officer: Jack Bishop

Executive Editorial Directors: Bridget Lancaster, Julia Collin Davison

CONTENTS

GETTING STARTED

Learn how to make great food for breakfast, lunch, dinner, and everything in between. In this book, you might see recipes for dishes you've already made a few times, and you might find recipes for dishes that are totally new to you. Either way, we hope you'll want to make them again and again! Plus, this book is full of technique pages that show you key kitchen skills—with plenty of helpful videos demonstrating exactly how to do them. Master these skills, and you'll be on your way to being a pro in the kitchen.

This cookbook is kid tested and kid approved. That means that there are thousands of other kids just like you out there who made these recipes and shared them with their friends and family, loving the process and the results. When making this book, we had more than 15,000 kids testing the recipes, sending us feedback, and letting us know what worked well and what could use improvement. You'll see a handful of these recipe testers in the pages of this book. Thank you to everyone who helped make this book as delicious as possible!

Cooking is a science as well as an art. Don't be surprised if you have questions as you get going in the kitchen (never hesitate to ask a grown-up!), and don't worry if you make some mistakes (we've all been there, many times). Mistakes are an important part of the learning process in the kitchen.

But the most important thing to remember as you begin cooking is to have fun! Use this book to be creative, to try out new things, and to experiment. Be proud of everything you're about to accomplish.

HOW TO USE THIS BOOK

UNDERSTANDING THE SYMBOLS IN THIS BOOK

To help you find the right recipes for you, this book uses different symbols that quickly show the skill level for each recipe, as well as the type(s) of cooking required.

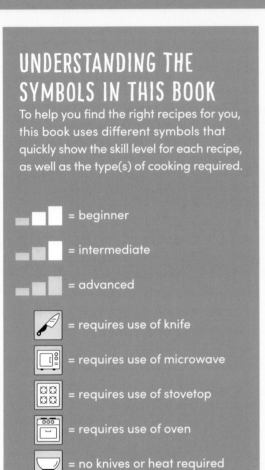

= beginner

= intermediate

= advanced

= requires use of knife

= requires use of microwave

= requires use of stovetop

= requires use of oven

= no knives or heat required

VIDEO TECHNIQUES

In some ingredient lists and recipe steps, you'll see a special play button: (▶). That means there's a video to help you see that technique in action—just go to the page number specified and use a tablet or smartphone to scan the QR code and watch the video. You'll see most of the QR codes on special technique pages, such as "The Basics: Chopping, Slicing, and Mincing" (page 92) and "The Basics: Get Organized!" (page 20).

THREE STEPS TO COOKING FROM A RECIPE

The key to successful (and easy!) cooking is, in our humble opinion, all about organization. To help you stay organized while you cook, the recipes in this book are broken down into three sections: "Prepare Ingredients," "Gather Cooking Equipment," and "Start Cooking!" If you prepare all your ingredients and gather all your equipment before you start cooking, then you won't have to run around the kitchen looking for that last pan or frantically measure out that last cup of flour while you're in the middle of stirring something on the stove.

PREPARE INGREDIENTS

Start with the list of ingredients and prepare them as directed. Measure ingredients, melt butter, and chop as needed. Wash fruits and vegetables. You can use small prep bowls to keep ingredients organized.

GATHER COOKING EQUIPMENT

Once all your ingredients are ready, put all the tools you will need to follow the recipe instructions on the counter.

START COOKING!

It's finally time to start cooking. Any ingredients that need to be prepped at the last minute will have instructions within the recipe itself. Don't forget to have fun!

SECRETS TO SUCCESS IN THE KITCHEN

Cooking isn't rocket science, but there are a few key strategies that will help make sure your recipes turn out great. Here are four secrets to becoming a kitchen pro.

SECRET #1: READ CAREFULLY

If you're learning to cook, chances are you are reading a recipe. It will take some time to understand the language used in recipes (see "Decoding Kitchenspeak," page 10). Before you do anything else, always read the entire recipe, from start to finish.

- Start with the key stats. How much food does the recipe make? How long will it take? When you're hungry for an after-school snack, choose a recipe that takes 30 minutes to prepare rather than an hour or two.

- Make sure that you have the right ingredients and equipment. Don't start a cupcake recipe only to realize you don't have any flour in your pantry. Likewise, don't prepare the ingredients for a recipe before making sure that you have the right equipment on hand.

- Follow the recipe as written, at least the first time. You can always improvise once you understand how the recipe works. See the "Try It This Way!" and "Make It Your Way!" sections for suggestions on how to customize recipes just the way you like them.

SECRET #2: STAY FOCUSED

While you're cooking, it's important that you're paying attention every step of the way.

- Measure carefully (see page 188 for tips). Adding too much salt can ruin a recipe. Too little baking powder can leave you with flat cakes and cookies.

- Recipes are written with both visual cues ("cook until golden brown") and times ("cook for 5 minutes"). Pay attention to both! Good cooks use all their senses—sight, hearing, touch, smell, and taste—in the kitchen.

- Many recipes contain time ranges, such as "cook until golden brown, 20 to 25 minutes." These ranges account for differences in various stovetops or ovens. Set your timer for the lower number. If the food isn't done when the timer goes off, you can always keep cooking and reset the timer. But once food is overcooked, there's no going back.

SECRET #3: PRACTICE SAFETY

Yes, knives and stoves can be dangerous. Always ask an adult for help if you're in doubt.

- Use the knife that's right for you. This will depend on the size of your hands and your skill level (see page 82 for recommendations).

- Hot stovetops and ovens can cause painful burns. Assume that anything on the stovetop (including the pan's handle and lid) is hot. Everything inside the oven is definitely hot, so always use oven mitts.

- Wash your hands before cooking.

- Wash your hands after touching raw chicken, turkey, beef, pork, fish, or eggs.

- Never let foods you eat raw (such as berries) touch foods you will cook (such as raw eggs).

- Don't ever leave something on the stove unattended. Always turn off the stove and oven when you're done.

SECRET #4: MISTAKES ARE OK

Making mistakes is a great way to learn, and they happen to literally everyone in the kitchen, at one time or another. Don't sweat it.

- Try to figure out what you would do differently next time. Maybe you should have set a timer so that you would have remembered to check the cookies in the oven, or maybe you should have measured more carefully.

- If your food isn't perfect, don't worry. A misshapen cookie is still delicious. If you enjoy your "mistakes," everyone else will enjoy them, too. Remember: You cooked! That's so cool.

DECODING KITCHENSPEAK

Reading a recipe can sometimes feel like reading another language. Here are some common words in many recipes and what they mean.

THINGS YOU DO WITH A SHARP TOOL

PEEL: To remove the outer skin, rind, or layer from food, usually a piece of fruit or a vegetable. Often done with a vegetable peeler.

ZEST: To remove the flavorful colored outer peel from a lemon, lime, or orange (the colored skin is called the zest). Does not include the bitter white layer (called the pith) under the zest.

CHOP: To cut food with a knife into small pieces.

MINCE: To cut food with a knife into ⅛-inch pieces or smaller.

SLICE: To cut food with a knife into pieces with two flat sides, with the thickness dependent on the recipe instructions. For example, slicing an onion.

GRATE: To cut food (often cheese) into very small, uniform pieces using a rasp grater or the small holes on a box grater.

SHRED: To cut food (often cheese, but also some vegetables and fruits) into small, uniform pieces using the large holes on a box grater or the shredding disk of a food processor.

THINGS YOU DO IN A BOWL

STIR: To combine ingredients in a bowl or cooking vessel, often with a rubber spatula or wooden spoon.

TOSS: To gently combine ingredients with tongs or two forks and/or spoons in order to distribute the ingredients evenly. You toss salad in a bowl (you don't stir it).

WHISK: To combine ingredients with a whisk until they're uniform or evenly incorporated. For example, you whisk whole eggs before scrambling them.

BEAT: To combine vigorously with a whisk, fork, or electric mixer, often with the goal of adding air to increase the volume of the ingredients (such as beating butter and sugar together to make cookie dough).

WHIP: To combine vigorously with a whisk or electric mixer, always with the goal of adding air to increase the volume of the ingredients (such as whipping cream or egg whites).

SCRAPE: To push ingredients from the sides of a bowl, pan, blender jar, or food processor back into the center. A rubber spatula is the best tool for this job.

THINGS YOU DO WITH HEAT

MELT: To heat solid food (such as butter) on the stovetop or in the microwave until it becomes a liquid.

SIMMER: To heat liquid until small bubbles break often across its surface, as when cooking a soup or sauce.

BOIL: To heat liquid until large bubbles break the surface at a rapid and constant rate, as when cooking pasta.

SHIMMER: To heat oil in a pan on the stovetop until it begins to move slightly, with little waves on the surface. This indicates that the oil is hot enough for cooking.

JUST SMOKING: To heat oil in a pan on the stovetop until you start to see wisps of smoke coming up from the oil. (You may need to get eye level with the pan to see this.) Turn on your stove's hood vent, if you have one.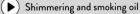

TOAST: To heat food (often nuts or bread) in a skillet, toaster, or oven until it's golden brown and fragrant.

VIDEO

Shimmering and smoking oil

ESSENTIAL PREP STEPS AND TECHNIQUES

Technique pages throughout this book teach you important kitchen skills. Here are a few more techniques you'll use often while cooking. (And don't forget, means there's a video to show you that skill!)

HOW TO SOFTEN BUTTER

When taken straight from the refrigerator, butter is quite firm. For some baking recipes, you need to soften butter before combining it with other ingredients. This is just a fancy term for letting the temperature of butter rise from 35 degrees (its refrigerator temperature) to 65 degrees (cool room temperature). This takes about 1 hour, but here are two ways to speed things up.

Counter Method: Cut butter into 1-inch pieces (to create more surface area). Place butter on plate and wait about 30 minutes. Once butter gives to light pressure (try to push your fingertip into butter), it's ready to use.

Microwave Method: Cut butter into 1-inch pieces and place on microwave-safe plate. Heat in microwave at 50 percent power (see "Microwave 101," right) for 10 seconds. Check butter with fingertip test. Heat for another 5 to 10 seconds if necessary.

HOW TO MELT BUTTER

Butter can be melted in a small saucepan on the stove (use medium-low heat), but we think the microwave is easier.

Cut butter into 1-tablespoon pieces. Place butter in microwave-safe bowl. Cover bowl with microwave-safe plate. Place in microwave. Heat butter at 50 percent power (see "Microwave 101," right) until melted, 30 to 60 seconds (longer if melting a lot of butter). Watch butter and stop microwave as soon as butter has melted. Use oven mitts to remove bowl from microwave.

HOW TO GRATE OR SHRED CHEESE ▶

Cheese is often cut into very small pieces before you add it to pizza, pasta, tacos, and more. When grating or shredding, use a big piece of cheese so that your hand stays safely away from the sharp holes.

1. To grate: Hard cheeses, such as Parmesan, can be rubbed against a rasp grater or the small holes of a box grater to make a fluffy pile of cheese.

2. To shred: Semisoft cheeses, such as cheddar or mozzarella, can be rubbed against the large holes of a box grater to make long pieces of cheese.

MICROWAVE 101

Most microwaves have a power setting that lets you cook things at reduced power levels. It's important to melt butter and chocolate at 50 percent of full power so it doesn't splatter and make a mess, or worse, burn! The controls can vary from microwave to microwave, but often you have to set the power level before setting the time. Ask an adult for help.

DON'T OVERMIX BATTER

To keep muffins and pancakes as light and tender as possible, the key is to not overmix the batter. This means mixing until the ingredients are just combined—the batter probably won't be completely smooth. Why? The more you mix, the more the proteins in the flour link up to form gluten. And the more gluten, the chewier and tougher the final product.

VIDEOS

 Melting butter

 Softening butter

Grating and shredding cheese

HOW TO ZEST AND JUICE CITRUS ▶

The flavorful colored skin from citrus fruits, such as lemons, limes, and oranges (called the zest), is often removed and used in recipes. If you need zest, it's best to zest before juicing. After juicing, use a small spoon to remove any seeds from the bowl of juice.

1. To zest: Rub fruit against rasp grater to remove colored zest. Turn fruit as you go to avoid bitter white layer underneath zest.

2. To juice: Use chef's knife to cut fruit in half through equator (not through ends).

3. Place 1 half of fruit in citrus juicer. Hold juicer over bowl and squeeze to extract juice.

HOW TO PEEL, GRATE, AND SLICE GINGER ▶

1. To peel: Place ginger on cutting board and hold firmly with 1 hand. Use vegetable peeler to peel off brown outer layer of ginger, peeling away from you.

2. To grate: Rub peeled ginger back and forth against rasp grater.

3. To slice: Use chef's knife to thinly slice peeled ginger crosswise (the short way).

HOW TO PREP AN AVOCADO ▶

1. Use butter knife or chef's knife to cut avocado in half lengthwise (the long way) around pit.

2. Using your hands, twist both halves in opposite directions to separate.

3. Use spoon to scoop out pit; discard pit.

4. Use spoon to scoop out avocado from skin; discard skin. Avocado can now be sliced, chopped, or mashed.

HOW TO TEST FOR DONENESS WITH A TOOTHPICK

Some recipes tell you to test a baked good for doneness with a toothpick. They will tell you if the toothpick should come out clean, or if a few crumbs stuck to it (see photos, below) are OK. If you see wet, sticky batter, keep baking.

clean ⎯   crumbs attached

To check: Insert toothpick into center of baked good, then remove it. Examine toothpick for crumbs and compare with directions in specific recipe to determine if baked good is ready to come out of oven.

VIDEOS

▶ Zesting and juicing citrus

▶ Peeling, grating, and slicing ginger

▶ Prepping avocado

ESSENTIAL KITCHEN GEAR

Here is the equipment you'll use over and over again in the kitchen, from small appliances to prep tools to knives and more.

KNIVES

Chef's knife

Paring knife

Cutting board

SMALL APPLIANCES

Electric hand mixer

Food processor

Blender

Stand mixer

COOKWARE & BAKEWARE

Traditional skillet (12-inch)

Nonstick skillets (12-inch and 10-inch)

8½-by-4½-inch metal loaf pan

Cooling rack

Large saucepan (3 to 4 quarts)

Dutch oven (6 to 7 quarts)

Muffin tins (12-cup and 24-cup mini)

Rimmed baking sheet

KITCHEN BASICS

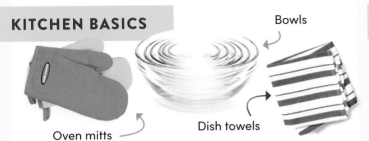

Bowls

Oven mitts

Dish towels

PREP TOOLS

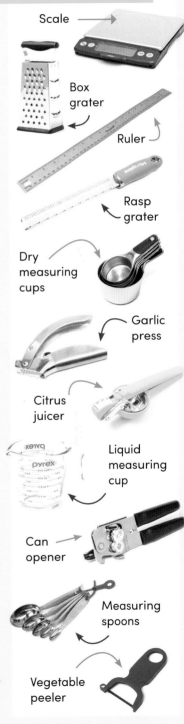

Scale

Box grater

Ruler

Rasp grater

Dry measuring cups

Garlic press

Citrus juicer

Liquid measuring cup

Can opener

Measuring spoons

Vegetable peeler

COOKING & BAKING TOOLS

Instant-read thermometer

Rubber spatula

Wooden spoon

Whisk

Spatula

Tongs

Ladle

Pastry brush

Fine-mesh strainer

Colander

Icing (offset) spatula

Bench scraper

Rolling pin

1 BREAKFAST

GET ORGANIZED!

Being organized is key to successful cooking. It helps you stay focused and makes sure that you don't miss anything as you go.

1 **READ THE ENTIRE RECIPE!**

Be sure to read through the whole recipe before you start— you don't want any surprises while you're cooking!

2 **TIE YOUR HAIR BACK**

Nobody wants to eat your hair!

3 **WASH YOUR HANDS**

It's essential to have clean hands before you start cooking. Also: Make sure to wash your hands after you touch raw meat, fish, or eggs.

4 **PREPARE YOUR INGREDIENTS**

"Mise en place" is the French term for "everything in its place," and it means exactly that: Prepare all the ingredients you'll need for your recipe before you start cooking. We like to put them in small "mise" bowls on the counter.

6 CLEAN AS YOU GO

It's not just your grown-ups nagging you—cleaning as you go also makes cooking easier, and it means that you'll have fewer dishes to wash after you eat. If there is downtime in a recipe (such as during baking or simmering), wash your dirty dishes and wipe down the counter.

5 GATHER YOUR EQUIPMENT

Make sure that you have all the equipment you need ready to go so that you're not searching for your tongs while your chicken is burning on the stove.

PUMPKIN MUFFINS

PREPARE INGREDIENTS

   Vegetable oil spray

2 cups (10 ounces) all-purpose flour

2 teaspoons baking powder

1 teaspoon baking soda

1 teaspoon table salt

¼ teaspoon ground allspice

¼ teaspoon ground ginger

2 teaspoons plus 1 teaspoon ground cinnamon, measured separately

1 (15-ounce) can unsweetened pumpkin puree, opened

¾ cup vegetable oil

2 large eggs

1½ cups (10½ ounces) plus 1 tablespoon sugar, measured separately

GATHER COOKING EQUIPMENT

12-cup muffin tin

3 bowls (1 large, 1 medium, 1 small)

Whisk

Rubber spatula

⅓-cup dry measuring cup

Spoon

Toothpick

Oven mitts

Cooling rack

MAKES 12 muffins

TOTAL TIME 1 hour, plus cooling time

LEVEL ◼️◻️◻️

"The crunchy top part with the cinnamon and sugar was my favorite part." —Brielle, 8

1 Adjust oven rack to middle position and heat oven to 375 degrees. Spray 12-cup muffin tin with vegetable oil spray.

2 In medium bowl, whisk together flour, baking powder, baking soda, salt, allspice, ginger, and 2 teaspoons cinnamon. In large bowl, whisk pumpkin, oil, eggs, and 1½ cups sugar until well combined.

3 Add flour mixture to pumpkin mixture and stir gently with rubber spatula until just combined and no dry flour is visible. Do not overmix (see page 13).

4 Use ⅓-cup dry measuring cup to divide batter evenly among muffin cups (use rubber spatula to scrape batter from cups if needed; see page 175).

5 In small bowl, use spoon to stir together remaining 1 tablespoon sugar and remaining 1 teaspoon cinnamon until combined. Sprinkle cinnamon-sugar mixture evenly over batter in each muffin cup.

6 Place muffin tin in oven. Bake until muffins are golden brown and toothpick inserted in center of 1 muffin comes out clean (see page 15), 20 to 25 minutes.

7 Use oven mitts to remove muffin tin from oven and place on cooling rack (ask an adult for help). Let muffins cool in muffin tin for 15 minutes.

8 Using your fingertips, gently wiggle muffins to loosen from muffin tin and transfer directly to cooling rack (see photo, right). Let muffins cool for at least 10 minutes before serving.

NO WAY, THAT'S PUMPKIN PUREE?

Spoiler alert: Canned pumpkin puree isn't made from jack-o'-lantern pumpkins, and most of the time, it actually isn't made from round, orange-skinned pumpkins at all! According to botanists (scientists who study plants), a pumpkin is any squash with a firm shell, a round body, and golden flesh. There are lots of squashes that check those boxes, including Dickinson squash, Hubbard squash, and even butternut squash. Canned pumpkin manufacturers will often use one or more of these sweet-tasting pumpkins to make their products. How do they go from patch to puree? The squashes are cleaned, mashed, strained, packed in cans, and—finally—cooked.

HOW TO REMOVE MUFFINS FROM A MUFFIN TIN

Using your fingertips, gently wiggle the muffins to help them slide out easily from the muffin tin. If they get stuck, use a butter knife to loosen their edges from the muffin tin. Transfer the muffins directly to a cooling rack.

BUTTERMILK PANCAKES

If you have an electric griddle, it's perfect for this recipe. Set the griddle to 350 degrees and cook all your pancakes in one batch.

PREPARE INGREDIENTS

1¼	cups all-purpose flour
1	tablespoon sugar
½	teaspoon baking powder
¼	teaspoon baking soda
¼	teaspoon table salt
1¼	cups buttermilk
1	large egg
3	tablespoons unsalted butter, melted and cooled (see page 12) ▶
2	tablespoons sour cream
	Vegetable oil spray

GATHER COOKING EQUIPMENT

2 bowls (1 large, 1 medium)

Whisk

Rubber spatula

12-inch nonstick skillet

¼-cup dry measuring cup

Spatula

Serving plates

SERVES 2 to 4 (Makes 8 pancakes)

TOTAL TIME 45 minutes

LEVEL ◼◼☐

START COOKING!

1 In large bowl, whisk together flour, sugar, baking powder, baking soda, and salt. In medium bowl, whisk buttermilk, egg, melted butter, and sour cream until well combined.

2 Add buttermilk mixture to flour mixture and stir gently with rubber spatula until just combined (batter should remain lumpy). Let batter sit for 10 minutes before cooking.

3 Spray 12-inch nonstick skillet with vegetable oil spray and heat over medium heat for 2 minutes (skillet should be hot but not smoking).

4 Scoop ¼ cup batter into skillet. Spread batter into 4-inch circle. Repeat 2 more times, leaving space between circles of batter (you want 3 pancakes with space to cook separate from one another).

5 Cook until bubbles form on surface of pancakes and begin to pop, 2 to 3 minutes.

6 Use spatula to flip pancakes. Cook until golden brown on second side, 1 to 2 minutes. Transfer pancakes to serving plate. Repeat with remaining batter in 2 more batches, turning down heat slightly if pancakes are getting very dark. Turn off heat. Serve.

BUTTERMILK MAKES ALL STACKS TALL STACKS

Traditionally, buttermilk is the liquid that's left over after cream is churned into butter (though the buttermilk you buy at the supermarket is made from pasteurized milk with harmless bacteria added to it). Buttermilk is acidic, similar to lemon juice and vinegar. When buttermilk comes into contact with baking soda, it forms bubbly carbon dioxide gas. Those gas bubbles create a network of tiny air pockets as these pancakes cook, giving them their height—and their fluffy, airy texture. You'll also see buttermilk (and baking soda) helping other baked goods, such as our Cinnamon-Raisin Swirl Bread (page 32), "rise" to the occasion.

MAKE IT YOUR WAY!

These pancakes are delicious with just butter and maple syrup, but you can also customize them with your favorite add-ins. At the end of step 4, sprinkle each pancake with 1 tablespoon of your chosen add-in, such as blueberries or raspberries, chopped strawberries, sliced bananas or apples, chocolate chips, chopped nuts, or shredded coconut. Sprinkling these ingredients onto each pancake as it cooks, instead of mixing them into the batter, makes sure that they're evenly distributed.

WAFFLES

Try serving these waffles with Apple-Cinnamon Syrup or Butter-Pecan Syrup (see right).

PREPARE INGREDIENTS

2	cups all-purpose flour
2	tablespoons sugar
1	tablespoon cream of tartar
2	teaspoons baking soda
1	teaspoon table salt
1½	cups milk
2	large eggs
4	tablespoons unsalted butter, melted and cooled (see page 12) ▶
	Vegetable oil spray

GATHER COOKING EQUIPMENT

2 bowls (1 large, 1 medium)

Whisk

Rubber spatula

Waffle iron

Dry measuring cups

Fork

Serving plates

SERVES 2 to 4 (Makes four 7-inch round waffles or two 9-inch square waffles)

TOTAL TIME 30 minutes

LEVEL ◼◻◻

"The waffles were soft and fluffy. I tried the Butter-Pecan Syrup, and it was the best sauce I've had."
—Grady, 9

1. In large bowl, whisk together flour, sugar, cream of tartar, baking soda, and salt. In medium bowl, whisk milk, eggs, and melted butter until well combined.

2. Add milk mixture to flour mixture and stir gently with rubber spatula until no dry flour is visible.

3. Heat waffle iron. When waffle iron is hot, spray lightly with vegetable oil spray. Use dry measuring cups and rubber spatula to scoop batter into middle of waffle iron (use about 1 cup batter for 7-inch round waffle iron or about 1½ cups batter for 9-inch square waffle iron). Spread batter into even layer. Close waffle iron and cook until waffle is golden brown.

4. Use fork to transfer waffle to serving plate. Repeat cooking with remaining batter. Turn off waffle iron. Serve.

INTRODUCING CREAM OF TARTAR

While these waffles are made with the usual suspects—flour, sugar, butter, eggs—one ingredient might surprise you: cream of tartar, an acidic powder. In this recipe, cream of tartar serves as a stand-in for another common (and acidic) waffle ingredient: buttermilk. When cream of tartar and baking soda meet in our waffle batter, they produce bubbly carbon dioxide gas. Look closely at the batter—do you see any bubbles? Those bubbles are trapped in the waffles as they cook, making them light and fluffy on the inside.

FLAVORED SYRUPS

APPLE-CINNAMON SYRUP

In medium saucepan, combine ¾ cup maple syrup, 2 tablespoons apple jelly, ⅛ teaspoon ground cinnamon, and pinch table salt. Whisk until well combined. Bring mixture to simmer over medium heat (small bubbles should break often across surface of mixture). Cook, whisking occasionally, until slightly thickened, 5 to 7 minutes.

BUTTER-PECAN SYRUP

In medium saucepan, combine ¾ cup maple syrup, ¼ cup chopped pecans, 1 tablespoon unsalted butter, ⅛ teaspoon vanilla extract, ⅛ teaspoon ground cinnamon, and pinch table salt. Whisk until well combined. Cook mixture over medium heat, whisking occasionally, until slightly thickened, 5 to 7 minutes.

CHOCOLATE PASTRY PUFFS

You can thaw frozen puff pastry by keeping it in the refrigerator overnight or leaving it out on the counter for about 30 minutes. We developed this recipe with Ghirardelli 60% Cacao Bittersweet Chocolate Baking Bars, which break apart into 2-inch squares, but you can use whatever bittersweet or semisweet chocolate bars you like.

PREPARE INGREDIENTS

   All-purpose flour, for sprinkling on counter

1   (9½-by-9-inch) sheet frozen puff pastry, thawed

3   ounces bittersweet chocolate, broken into six 2-inch squares

1   large egg, cracked into bowl and lightly beaten with fork (see page 37)

1–2   teaspoons confectioners' (powdered) sugar

GATHER COOKING EQUIPMENT

   Rimmed baking sheet

   Parchment paper

   Rolling pin

   Ruler

   Bench scraper or chef's knife

   Pastry brush

   Oven mitts

   Cooling rack

   Fine-mesh strainer

   Small bowl

MAKES **6 pastries**

TOTAL TIME **50 minutes**

LEVEL ■■□□

"It made me feel like a professional baker."
—Kendall, 10

START COOKING!

1 Adjust oven rack to middle position and heat oven to 400 degrees. Line rimmed baking sheet with parchment paper.

2 Lightly sprinkle clean counter with flour. Unfold puff pastry onto floured counter. Use rolling pin to gently roll puff pastry into 10½-inch square.

3 Cut, fill, and shape pastries following photos, page 30.

4 Transfer shaped pastries to parchment-lined baking sheet, leaving space between pastries. Use pastry brush to paint tops of pastries evenly with beaten egg.

5 Place baking sheet in oven and bake until pastries are puffed and deep golden brown, about 20 minutes.

6 Use oven mitts to remove baking sheet from oven and place on cooling rack (ask an adult for help). Let pastries cool on baking sheet for 10 minutes.

7 Set fine-mesh strainer over small bowl. Add confectioners' sugar to strainer. Use fine-mesh strainer to dust confectioners' sugar evenly over pastries, gently tapping side of strainer to release sugar (see page 181). Serve warm.

KEEP GOING!

PUFF IT UP!

These breakfast treats are similar to pain au chocolat ("PAHN oh shock-uh-LAH"), a flaky French pastry with a chocolate center, but they're much simpler to make! We start with store-bought puff pastry, which is made of superthin layers of dough and butter. It puffs up in the oven as the water in the butter heats up and escapes as steam. To get the biggest puff in your pastries, follow these two tips.

USE A BENCH SCRAPER OR SHARP KNIFE A bench scraper or sharp knife will help you make clean cuts through the dough. A dull knife will pinch the edges of the dough shut, trapping steam and preventing maximum puff.

KEEP IT COOL You don't want the butter in the puff pastry to melt until the pastries are in the oven. Thawing the dough in the refrigerator overnight (or on the counter for just 30 minutes) keeps it from getting too warm.

HOW TO SHAPE PASTRY PUFFS

1 Use bench scraper to cut pastry into six 3½-by-5¼-inch rectangles.

2 Place 1 chocolate square in top half of each rectangle, leaving ¾-inch border.

3 Use pastry brush to paint edges of pastry with beaten egg on 3 sides around chocolate square.

4 Fold pastry in half over chocolate. Use your fingers to press edges of pastry to seal.

CINNAMON-RAISIN SWIRL BREAD

PREPARE INGREDIENTS

Vegetable oil spray

2 teaspoons ground cinnamon

6 tablespoons (2⅔ ounces) plus 1 cup (7 ounces) sugar, measured separately

3 cups (15 ounces) all-purpose flour

1½ teaspoons baking soda

¾ teaspoon table salt

1½ cups (12 ounces) buttermilk

⅓ cup vegetable oil

2 large eggs

½ cup raisins

GATHER COOKING EQUIPMENT

8½-by-4½-inch metal loaf pan

3 bowls (1 large, 1 medium, 1 small)

Whisk

Rubber spatula

Dry measuring cups

1-tablespoon measuring spoon

Butter knife

Toothpick

Oven mitts

Cooling rack

SERVES 10

TOTAL TIME 2 hours, plus 1¼ hours cooling time

LEVEL

START COOKING!

1 Adjust oven rack to middle position and heat oven to 325 degrees. Spray inside bottom and sides of 8½-by-4½-inch metal loaf pan with vegetable oil spray.

2 In small bowl, whisk together cinnamon and 6 tablespoons sugar. Set aside. In medium bowl, whisk together flour, baking soda, salt, and remaining 1 cup sugar.

3 In large bowl, whisk together buttermilk, oil, and eggs. Add flour mixture to buttermilk mixture and use rubber spatula to stir until just combined and no dry flour is visible. Add raisins and gently stir to combine. Do not overmix (see page 13).

4 Use measuring cups to layer and swirl batter and cinnamon-sugar mixture in greased loaf pan following photos, page 34.

5 Place loaf pan in oven. Bake until toothpick inserted in center of bread comes out clean (see page 15), 1 hour and 15 minutes to 1 hour and 25 minutes.

6 Use oven mitts to remove loaf pan from oven and place on cooling rack (ask an adult for help). Let bread cool in pan for 15 minutes.

7 Use oven mitts to carefully turn loaf pan on its side and remove bread from pan. Let bread cool on cooling rack for at least 1 hour before serving.

KEEP GOING!

QUICK(ER) BREADS

Lots of breads rely on yeast for their height, but yeast needs hours to make dough rise. What if you want to skip all that rising time? Quick breads, such as this one, are made with chemical leaveners—baking powder, baking soda, or a combination—instead of yeast. When baking soda comes into contact with an acidic liquid, such as lemon juice or buttermilk (see "Buttermilk Makes All Stacks Tall Stacks," page 25), it creates carbon dioxide gas. That gas causes batters and doughs to rise and gives quick breads and other baked goods, such as cakes and brownies, their height. Baking powder already contains an acid, so as soon as it comes into contact with a liquid, it gets to work creating carbon dioxide.

"I never knew baking bread could be so easy. I'm making more for my family."
—Jackson, 8

1 Measure 1½ cups batter into greased loaf pan (use rubber spatula to level batter and scrape it out of cups). Smooth batter into even layer. Sprinkle 2 tablespoons cinnamon sugar evenly over batter. Repeat layering 2 more times with remaining batter and cinnamon sugar (there will be 3 of each layer in total).

2 Insert butter knife into batter until tip touches bottom of loaf pan. Swirl cinnamon sugar and batter together, moving knife side to side and down length of pan. Make sure tip of knife touches pan bottom as you work. Smooth top of loaf into even layer.

COOKING EGGS

You can cook eggs so many different ways—scrambled, hard-cooked, soft-cooked, poached, fried, and more. Check out our recipes for eggs on pages 38, 40, and 42.

TWO INGREDIENTS IN ONE

Eggs are really two ingredients—a yolk and a white—that come in a single package, the shell. Egg whites and yolks contain different amounts of water, protein, and fat. That means that they react very differently to heat as you cook them—always pay attention to the cooking times in recipes.

Egg Whites

Egg whites start to change from liquid to solid when they reach about 145 degrees, and they are completely solid and ready to eat when they reach 180 degrees.

Egg Yolks

Egg yolks, on the other hand, start to become solid at 150 degrees and are completely solid at 158 degrees.

HOW TO CRACK AND SEPARATE AN EGG ▶

1 TO CRACK Gently hit side of egg against flat surface of counter or cutting board.

2 Pull shell apart into 2 pieces over bowl. Let yolk and white drop into bowl. Discard shell.

3 TO SEPARATE YOLK AND WHITE Use your fingers to very gently transfer yolk to second bowl, letting white fall through your fingers.

HOW TO LIGHTLY BEAT AN EGG

Sometimes a recipe calls for brushing an egg wash (a beaten egg) over dough. The layer of egg helps the dough brown, gives it a shiny top, and can also help seal two pieces of dough together.

Crack egg into bowl. Use fork to beat egg until well combined. Hint: Moving the fork quickly from side to side works better than moving it in a circle.

VIDEO

▶ Cracking and separating eggs

BREAKFAST QUESADILLAS

To thaw frozen tater tots, let them sit in the refrigerator for 24 hours or arrange them on a paper towel–lined plate and heat in the microwave for 1½ minutes. "Bulk" sausage doesn't have a casing (it looks like ground meat). If you can't find bulk breakfast sausage, you can cut open the casings of tube-shaped breakfast sausages, remove the meat, and discard the casings.

PREPARE INGREDIENTS

- 4 large eggs
- 1 tablespoon plus 1 tablespoon vegetable oil, measured separately
- 1½ cups (about 20) frozen tater tots, thawed
- 4 ounces bulk breakfast sausage
- 4 (8-inch) flour tortillas
- 1 cup shredded Monterey Jack cheese (4 ounces) (see page 13) ▶

GATHER COOKING EQUIPMENT

Large plate	Rimmed baking sheet
Paper towels	Pastry brush
Medium bowl	Oven mitts
Whisk	Cooling rack
12-inch nonstick skillet	Cutting board
Spatula	Chef's knife
Rubber spatula	

SERVES 4

TOTAL TIME 50 minutes

LEVEL ■■□

It was like heaven on a plate!" —Brooklyn, 10

1 Adjust oven rack to upper-middle position and heat oven to 450 degrees. Line large plate with double layer of paper towels. In medium bowl, whisk eggs until well combined and uniform yellow color.

2 In 12-inch nonstick skillet, heat 1 tablespoon oil over medium-high heat until shimmering, about 2 minutes (oil should be hot but not smoking; see page 11). ▶

3 Carefully add thawed tater tots to skillet. Use spatula to break up and flatten tater tots. Cook until crispy and deep golden brown on first side, about 4 minutes. Flip tater tots. Cook until crispy and deep golden brown on second side, 2 to 3 minutes. Turn off heat.

4 Use spatula to transfer tater tots to paper towel–lined plate.

5 Add sausage to now-empty skillet and cook over medium heat, breaking up meat with rubber spatula, until well browned, 4 to 6 minutes.

6 Add beaten eggs to skillet. Use rubber spatula to stir egg mixture until eggs have clumped and are still slightly wet, about 2 minutes (scrape bottom and sides of skillet several times as eggs cook). Turn off heat and slide skillet to cool burner.

7 Lay tortillas on rimmed baking sheet. Use pastry brush to paint tortillas with remaining 1 tablespoon oil. Flip tortillas so oiled sides are down.

8 Sprinkle cheese evenly over half of each tortilla. Use spatula to divide cooked tater tots and then egg mixture evenly over cheese (see photo, above right).

9 Fold tortillas in half, forming half-moon shape with fillings inside, and use spatula to press lightly to flatten.

10 Place baking sheet in oven and bake quesadillas until spotty brown, 5 to 7 minutes.

11 Use oven mitts to remove baking sheet from oven and place on cooling rack (ask an adult for help). Transfer quesadillas to cutting board. Let quesadillas cool for 5 minutes. Use chef's knife to cut into wedges and serve.

QUESADILLAS FOR EVERYONE!

Quesadillas are typically cooked on the stovetop, but you can't fit more than one or two in a skillet. To make quesadillas for your whole family, use the oven: Four quesadillas fit on a single rimmed baking sheet. Brushing the tortillas with oil helps them brown and crisp. And since the fillings inside these quesadillas are already cooked, they need just a few minutes in the oven to melt the cheese and brown the tortillas.

FANCY SCRAMBLED EGGS

PREPARE INGREDIENTS

3 large eggs plus 1 large egg yolk (see page 37) ▶

2 tablespoons half-and-half

Pinch table salt

Pinch pepper

1 tablespoon unsalted butter

GATHER COOKING EQUIPMENT

Medium bowl

Whisk

10-inch nonstick skillet

Rubber spatula

Serving plates

> "10 out of 10! These are some of the best eggs I have ever eaten!"
> —Maya, 10

SERVES 2

TOTAL TIME 15 minutes

LEVEL ■■□□

1   In medium bowl, combine eggs and egg yolk, half-and-half, salt, and pepper. Whisk until very well combined and uniform yellow color, about 30 seconds.

2   In 10-inch nonstick skillet, melt butter over medium-high heat, swirling evenly to coat skillet.

3   Add egg mixture to skillet and use rubber spatula to constantly and firmly scrape bottom and sides of skillet until eggs begin to clump and spatula leaves trail on bottom of skillet, 1 to 2 minutes.

4   Reduce heat to low. Use rubber spatula to gently and constantly stir eggs until clumped and slightly wet, 30 to 60 seconds. Turn off heat and slide skillet to cool burner. Transfer eggs to serving plates and serve.

A SUPER SCRAMBLE

Scrambled eggs are one of the simplest dishes to cook, but just a few easy tweaks can take your breakfast from regular to fancy. Adding a splash of half-and-half and an extra egg yolk—two ingredients that contain fat—gives this scramble its rich, creamy texture. Special molecules in egg yolks (called emulsifiers) also help prevent the eggs from overcooking and turning tough. Starting the eggs over medium-high heat quickly turns water in the egg mixture to steam, forming big, puffy curds. Then, dropping the heat to low and stirring constantly allows the eggs to set (turn from a liquid into a solid) without overcooking.

MAKE IT YOUR WAY!

You can customize your scrambled eggs with different add-ins. In the beginning of step 4, you can add 1 tablespoon chopped herbs (such as chives, parsley, or dill), 1 cup chopped baby spinach, ¼ cup quartered cherry tomatoes, or 2 tablespoons shredded cheese (such as cheddar or Monterey Jack).

EGGS IN A HOLE

If you don't have a round cutter, you can use a sturdy drinking glass to cut the holes in the toast.

PREPARE INGREDIENTS

2 slices hearty white or wheat sandwich bread

1 tablespoon unsalted butter, cut into 4 pieces and softened (see page 12) ▶

Vegetable oil spray

2 large eggs

⅛ teaspoon table salt

Pinch pepper

GATHER COOKING EQUIPMENT

Toaster

Butter knife

Cutting board

2½-inch round cutter

12-inch nonstick skillet with lid

Oven mitts

Spatula

Serving plates

"It is a cool way to get your eggs and toast together."
—Teresa, 11

SERVES 2

TOTAL TIME 30 minutes

LEVEL ▪▫▫

1 Place bread in toaster on lowest setting. Toast until bread feels dried out and is very light brown. (You may have to toast it twice.)

2 Use butter knife to spread 1 piece of softened butter evenly over 1 side of each piece of toast.

3 Place toast on cutting board, buttered side up. Use 2½-inch round cutter to cut and remove circle from center of each piece of toast. Reserve toast circles.

4 Spray 12-inch nonstick skillet evenly with vegetable oil spray. Place pieces of toast and reserved toast circles, buttered sides down, in skillet.

5 Place 1 piece of softened butter in hole of each piece of toast. Crack 1 egg into each hole (see photo, below right). Wash your hands. Sprinkle evenly with salt and pepper.

6 Cover skillet with lid and cook over medium-low heat until egg whites are set and yolks still jiggle, 8 to 10 minutes for slightly runny yolks or 9 to 11 minutes for set yolks.

7 Turn off heat and slide skillet to cool burner. Use oven mitts to remove lid. Use spatula to carefully transfer eggs in a hole and toast circles to plates. Serve.

MAKE IT YOUR WAY!

For a heartier breakfast, you can add toppings to your Eggs in a Hole. In step 6, after the eggs and toast have been cooking for 4 minutes, use oven mitts to carefully remove the lid from the skillet and sprinkle each piece of toast with ¼ ounce shredded cheddar or Monterey Jack cheese or ½ ounce diced deli ham or turkey. Replace the lid and continue to cook as directed.

"EGGSTRAORDINARY" SCIENCE

To crack the code for these Eggs in a Hole, we place the toast in a cold skillet and crack an egg into each hole before we turn on the stove. Putting a lid on the skillet traps hot steam inside the pan, so the eggs get a blast of heat from both the top and bottom. This helps the whites cook through more quickly and keeps the yolks from overcooking. Hello, quick and tasty breakfast!

HOW TO CRACK EGGS IN A HOLE

Crack 1 egg into each hole in toast, on top of butter.

BREAKFAST COOKIES

Do not use quick or instant oats in this recipe. You can swap almond butter or sunflower seed butter for the peanut butter, if desired. Note that cookies made with sunflower seed butter will be slightly softer.

PREPARE INGREDIENTS

- ½ cup (2½ ounces) all-purpose flour
- ¼ teaspoon table salt
- ¼ teaspoon baking soda
- ½ cup packed (3½ ounces) light brown sugar
- ¼ cup creamy peanut butter
- 1 large egg
- 2 tablespoons unsalted butter, melted and cooled (see page 12)
- ½ teaspoon vanilla extract
- ⅛ teaspoon ground cinnamon
- 1½ cups (4½ ounces) old-fashioned rolled oats
- ¼ cup dried cherries
- ¼ cup sliced almonds

GATHER COOKING EQUIPMENT

Rimmed baking sheet	Rubber spatula
Parchment paper	1-tablespoon measuring spoon
2 bowls (1 large, 1 medium)	Ruler
	Oven mitts
Whisk	Cooling rack

MAKES 12 cookies

TOTAL TIME 40 minutes, plus cooling time

LEVEL ■■□

"The peanut butter and the brown sugar make it chewy and the chewiness makes it yummy."
—Sadie, 9

1 Adjust oven rack to middle position and heat oven to 375 degrees. Line rimmed baking sheet with parchment paper.

2 In medium bowl, whisk together flour, salt, and baking soda. In large bowl, whisk brown sugar, peanut butter, egg, melted butter, vanilla, and cinnamon until smooth.

3 Add flour mixture to brown sugar mixture and use rubber spatula to stir until no dry flour is visible. Add oats, cherries, and almonds and stir until well combined.

4 Lightly wet your hands. Roll dough into 12 balls (about 2 tablespoons each). Place dough balls on parchment-lined baking sheet, leaving space between balls. Gently flatten dough balls following photo, below right. (Dough will be sticky; lightly re-wet your hands as needed while shaping cookies.)

5 Place baking sheet in oven. Bake cookies until edges are set but centers are still soft, 8 to 10 minutes.

6 Use oven mitts to remove baking sheet from oven and place on cooling rack (ask an adult for help). Let cookies cool completely on baking sheet, about 30 minutes. Serve.

TRY IT THIS WAY!

APRICOT-PEPITA BREAKFAST COOKIES

Use ¼ **cup chopped dried apricots** instead of dried cherries and ¼ **cup pepitas** instead of sliced almonds.

RAISIN–SUNFLOWER SEED BREAKFAST COOKIES

Use ¼ **cup raisins** instead of dried cherries and ¼ **cup sunflower seeds** instead of sliced almonds.

COOKIES . . . FOR BREAKFAST?!

You heard us right: These cookies are breakfast approved. So what makes them different from your typical dessert cookie? For starters, they're packed with hearty oats and protein-rich peanut butter for all-morning energy. Plus, a healthy dose of nuts and dried fruit bulks them up even more and adds crunchy, chewy texture. Eat your cookies at the breakfast table, or pack them in your lunch box for an on-the-go breakfast or energy-boosting snack.

HOW TO SHAPE BREAKFAST COOKIES

Lightly wet your hands and use your fingers to gently flatten each dough ball into 2½-inch-wide circle, about ¼ inch thick.

BLUEBERRY BAKED OATMEAL

Quick oats, also called 1-minute oats, stick together best in this baked oatmeal. You can use old-fashioned rolled oats instead, but the texture will be looser. Do not use steel-cut oats in this recipe.

PREPARE INGREDIENTS

    Vegetable oil spray

3 cups (9 ounces) quick oats

1 cup packed (7 ounces) brown sugar

2 teaspoons baking powder

1 teaspoon table salt

1 teaspoon ground cinnamon

1½ cups (12 ounces) milk, plus extra for serving

2 large eggs

6 tablespoons unsalted butter, melted (see page 12) ▶

1 cup blueberries

GATHER COOKING EQUIPMENT

    8-inch square baking dish

2 bowls (1 large, 1 medium)

Whisk

Rubber spatula

Oven mitts

Cooling rack

Serving bowls

SERVES 8

TOTAL TIME 1¼ hours

LEVEL ◼◻◻

"I can't wait to try this recipe hot out of the oven after sledding."
—Anna, 12

START COOKING!

1. Adjust oven rack to middle position and heat oven to 350 degrees. Spray inside bottom and sides of 8-inch square baking dish with vegetable oil spray.

2. In large bowl, whisk together oats, brown sugar, baking powder, salt, and cinnamon. In medium bowl, whisk milk, eggs, and melted butter until well combined.

3. Add milk mixture to oat mixture and stir with rubber spatula until well combined. Gently stir in blueberries. Transfer mixture to greased baking dish and spread into even layer.

4. Place baking dish in oven. Bake until oatmeal is set and edges are golden brown, 40 to 45 minutes.

5. Use oven mitts to remove baking dish from oven and place on cooling rack (ask an adult for help). Let oatmeal cool on rack for at least 10 minutes.

6. Scoop baked oatmeal into serving bowls. Pour a little extra milk over baked oatmeal in each bowl. Serve warm. (Baked oatmeal can be cooled to room temperature, covered with plastic wrap, and refrigerated for up to 5 days. Reheat individual portions in microwave for 1 to 2 minutes.)

DON'T MISS "OAT" ON BAKED OATMEAL

Sure, you can cook oatmeal on the stovetop or in the microwave, but if you bake oatmeal with a handful of extra ingredients (such as eggs, milk, and baking powder), you'll get a delicious, cake-like breakfast, with crispy edges and a soft, tender interior. Using quick oats here is key—quick oats are especially good at sticking together when cooked (unlike old-fashioned or steel-cut oats), so you can easily scoop your breakfast into a bowl. Top your baked oatmeal with a splash of milk and some toppings, and you just might have your new favorite breakfast.

MAKE IT YOUR WAY!

You can top your portion of baked oatmeal with a drizzle of maple syrup, more fresh berries, sliced apples or bananas, raisins or dried cranberries, and/or a sprinkle of chopped nuts or shredded coconut.

2 SNACKS

CHILI-LIME TROPICAL TRAIL MIX

PREPARE INGREDIENTS

1 tablespoon grated lime zest plus 2 tablespoons juice, zested and squeezed from 2 limes (see page 14)

2 teaspoons extra-virgin olive oil

2 teaspoons sugar

1–2 teaspoons chili powder

¾ teaspoon table salt

2 cups whole almonds, cashews, or pecans

½ cup unsweetened coconut flakes

½ cup dried pineapple tidbits

½ cup semisweet or white chocolate chips

GATHER COOKING EQUIPMENT

2 bowls (1 large, 1 medium)

Rubber spatula

12-inch nonstick skillet

Large plate

MAKES 3½ cups

TOTAL TIME 35 minutes, plus cooling time

LEVEL ◼◼◻

START COOKING!

1   In medium bowl, combine lime zest and juice, oil, sugar, chili powder, and salt. Use rubber spatula to stir until well combined. Add almonds to bowl and stir until evenly coated with spice mixture.

2   Scrape almonds and spice mixture into 12-inch nonstick skillet. Cook over medium-low heat, stirring frequently, until liquid has evaporated and almonds are fragrant and sizzling, 7 to 10 minutes (almonds will still look slightly wet). Turn off heat.

3   Transfer almonds to large plate. Spread into even layer and let cool completely, about 30 minutes.

4   In large bowl, use rubber spatula to stir cooled almonds, coconut flakes, pineapple tidbits, and chocolate chips until combined. Serve. (Trail mix can be stored in airtight container for up to 4 days.)

SPICE UP YOUR TRAIL MIX

We wanted a trail mix that not only has the usual combination of nuts, dried fruit, and chocolate but also has a TON of extra flavor. To make sure that each and every nut in our trail mix is fully coated with chili-lime seasoning, we first toss the raw nuts with a mixture of lime zest and juice, olive oil, salt, sugar, and chili powder. The salt and sugar dissolve in the watery lime juice, which also helps evenly distribute the chili powder and zest. As the nuts toast in the hot skillet, the water in the lime juice evaporates, leaving behind a flavor-packed coating.

"It was, like, WOW! I loved the way the different flavors blended together!"
—Cat, 11

GARLIC-SESAME NORI CHIPS

The less-shiny, rough sides of nori sheets stick together better than the very shiny, smooth sides. Not sure which side is which? Run your hand lightly over the nori sheet to see if it feels rough or smooth.

PREPARE INGREDIENTS

- 2 teaspoons sesame seeds
- ¼ teaspoon garlic powder
- ¼ teaspoon kosher salt
-   Pinch cayenne pepper (optional)
- 4 (8-by-7½-inch) sheets nori
- 2 tablespoons water
- 1 tablespoon toasted sesame oil

GATHER COOKING EQUIPMENT

- Rimmed baking sheet
- Parchment paper
- Small bowl
- Spoon
- Pastry brush
- ¼-teaspoon measuring spoon
- Kitchen shears
- Oven mitts
- Cooling rack

SERVES 2 to 4

TOTAL TIME 50 minutes

LEVEL ▪▪▫

"Very fast, very easy, very crispy, and very tasty!"
—Audrey, 13

1   Adjust oven rack to middle position and heat oven to 350 degrees. Line rimmed baking sheet with parchment paper.

2   In small bowl, combine sesame seeds, garlic powder, salt, and cayenne (if using). Use spoon to stir until well combined.

3   Shape nori sheets into triangles and season following photos, page 54.

4   Transfer nori triangles, seasoned side up, to parchment-lined baking sheet.

5   Place baking sheet in oven. Bake until chips are slightly shriveled and sesame seeds are golden, about 8 minutes.

6   Use oven mitts to remove baking sheet from oven and place on cooling rack (ask an adult for help). Let chips cool on baking sheet for 10 minutes. Serve.

KEEP GOING! →

KNOW YOUR NORI

Nori is a mild-flavored seaweed used in all sorts of Japanese dishes. But it doesn't grow in flat, even rectangles! To make nori sheets, moist, wavy, raw nori is cleaned, minced, pressed, and dried into flat, crisp sheets. To up the crispness and make our nori chips sturdier, we fold each sheet in half before baking, using water to stick the folded sheet together. Painting each nori sheet with toasted sesame oil adds even more chip-like crunch and helps the sesame seed mixture stick.

HOW TO SHAPE AND SEASON NORI CHIPS

1 Place 1 nori sheet, shiny side down, on clean counter. Use pastry brush to paint bottom half of nori sheet with water (nori should be wet, but not soaked). Fold top half toward you and press firmly to seal.

2 Paint top of folded nori sheet lightly with sesame oil. Sprinkle ¼ teaspoon sesame seed mixture evenly over top.

3 Use kitchen shears to cut folded nori sheet in half crosswise (the short way) to make 2 squares.

4 Cut each square in half diagonally to make 2 triangles. Cut each triangle in half to make 2 smaller triangles. You should have 8 small triangles. Repeat steps 1 through 4 with remaining nori, water, oil, and sesame seed mixture.

WATERMELON-MANGO SKEWERS WITH TAJÍN

You can use precut watermelon and mango sold in containers at the grocery store for this recipe, or ask an adult to help you peel and prep the fruit before cutting it into 1-inch pieces. We used Tajín Clásico when developing this recipe; you can find it in the Latin section of most grocery stores or in Latin markets. If you can't find it, look for "chili-lime salt" in the spice aisle.

PREPARE INGREDIENTS

- 2 tablespoons lime juice, squeezed from 1 lime (see page 14) ▶
- 1 teaspoon sugar
- ¼ teaspoon table salt
- 12 ounces seedless watermelon, cut into 24 (1-inch) pieces
- 8 ounces mango, cut into 24 (1-inch) pieces
- 24 fresh mint leaves (optional)
- 1–2 teaspoons Tajín seasoning

GATHER COOKING EQUIPMENT

- Large bowl
- Rubber spatula
- 8 (10-inch) wooden skewers
- Serving platter

SERVES 4

TOTAL TIME 30 minutes

LEVEL ▢

START COOKING!

1 In large bowl, use rubber spatula to stir lime juice, sugar, and salt until sugar and salt dissolve. Add watermelon and mango and stir until fruit is coated. Let sit for 5 minutes.

2 Assemble fruit skewer following photo, right. Repeat with remaining fruit and mint (if using) to make 8 skewers total.

3 Place skewers on serving platter. Sprinkle evenly with Tajín on all sides. Serve.

HOW TO SKEWER FRUIT

Slide watermelon piece onto wooden skewer. Slide mint leaf (if using) onto skewer, then slide mango piece onto skewer. Repeat pattern two more times for 6 pieces of fruit and 3 mint leaves total.

SPICE IS NICE

The flavor combination of chile peppers and lime is so popular in Mexican cuisine that one company turned it into a seasoning blend that you can sprinkle on just about anything: Tajín! Tajín ("ta-HEEN") is made from ground mild red chile peppers, sea salt, and dried lime. It has a salty, sour, and slightly spicy flavor that's not only delicious sprinkled on sweet fresh fruit, but also tastes great on corn, eggs, avocado toast, roasted veggies, and more.

SEASONING AND SPICES

We use salt to season almost every recipe in this book, and spices pack a ton of flavor into every teaspoon. Here, you'll learn how to make the most of these important ingredients.

Salt High

If you've ever seen a chef sprinkle salt, you may have noticed that they hold their hand way up high. Sprinkling from up high helps the salt cover the food more evenly.

HOW TO SEASON TO TASTE

When you finish a recipe, take a tiny taste. Is it bland? Could it use more flavor? Add a pinch of salt, stir if necessary, and taste again. Repeat until you're happy with the dish. Remember to add only a tiny bit of salt at a time—you can always add more, but there's not much you can do to fix something that's too salty!

WHICH TYPE OF SALT SHOULD I USE?

There are three varieties of salt that we cook with: table salt, kosher salt, and sea salt. Here are some tips about when to use each type and how to tell them apart.

Table Salt

- Tiny, uniform-size salt crystals
- Dissolves easily in liquids
- Good for brining and baking

Kosher Salt

- Small, coarse flakes of different sizes
- Sticks well to food
- Good for seasoning meat, fish, and vegetables

Sea Salt

- Large flakes of different sizes
- Adds flavor and texture
- Good for sprinkling on food right before you eat it

SMELLY SPICES

Most of a spice's flavor actually comes from its aroma, or smell. Our noses detect tiny aroma molecules that spices release into the air. Spices are chock-full of aroma molecules, which is why just a little bit of spice gives you a lot of flavor!

BLOOMING SPICES

Some recipes, such as Spiced Red Lentil Soup (page 100) and Loaded Nachos (page 64), call for cooking spices in hot oil or butter before adding other ingredients. This technique is called "blooming" the spices. Blooming actually changes the flavor of the spice—and the flavor of the butter or oil, too.

SPICE OR HERB?

Plants not only provide us with spices. They also give us another flavor-packed type of ingredient: herbs, such as thyme, rosemary, and cilantro. Herbs come from the leaves and stems of plants. A recipe might call for fresh herbs (learn more on page 66) or dried herbs, which are usually sold in the spice aisle of the grocery store.

Two Types of Spice

Many spices are sold whole, such as cinnamon sticks, nutmeg, and black peppercorns. Whole spices can be crushed—by hand or using a machine—and turned into powdery ground spices, such as ground ginger, ground cumin, or chili powder.

EDAMAME WITH LEMON-PEPPER SALT

This recipe makes extra flavored salt—try sprinkling it on popcorn, chicken, fish, or more edamame!

PREPARE INGREDIENTS

¼ cup kosher salt

2 teaspoons grated lemon zest plus 2 tablespoons juice, zested and squeezed from 1 lemon (see page 14) ▶

½ teaspoon pepper

2 quarts water, plus extra cold water for cooling edamame

12 ounces frozen shell-on edamame

GATHER COOKING EQUIPMENT

2 bowls (1 large, 1 small)

Spoon

Microwave-safe plate

Oven mitts

Colander

Large saucepan

Spider skimmer or slotted spoon

Dish towel

1-tablespoon measuring spoon

Rubber spatula

SERVES 4

TOTAL TIME 30 minutes

LEVEL ■■□□

1   In small bowl, use spoon to stir salt, lemon zest and juice, and pepper until well combined. Transfer to microwave-safe plate and use back of spoon to spread into even layer.

2   Place plate in microwave and heat for 1 minute. Stir and scrape mixture, breaking up any clumps, and spread back into even layer. Continue heating in microwave until mixture is only slightly damp, 1 to 3 minutes, stopping and stirring after each minute of heating.

3   Use oven mitts to remove plate from microwave. Let salt mixture cool completely, about 10 minutes.

4   Meanwhile, fill large bowl halfway with cold water and set next to stove. Set colander in sink.

5   Add 2 quarts water to large saucepan and bring to boil over high heat. Carefully add edamame (ask an adult for help). Return to boil and cook until tender, about 3 minutes. Turn off heat.

6   Use spider skimmer to transfer edamame to bowl with cold water. Let sit for 30 seconds to cool slightly.

7   Pour edamame into colander and let drain in sink. Use dish towel to dry now-empty large bowl. Shake colander to drain well. Transfer drained edamame to bowl.

8   Sprinkle edamame with 1 tablespoon lemon-pepper salt. Use rubber spatula to stir until edamame are evenly coated. Serve, using your teeth to gently squeeze beans out of edamame pods and into your mouth (discard pods). (Extra flavored salt can be stored in an airtight container for up to 1 month.)

EDAMAME WORTH ITS (FANCY) SALT

Fancy flavored salt adds some oomph to plain edamame. We start by combining lemon zest, black pepper, and enough lemon juice to wet the salt crystals—but not so much that the salt dissolves. Heating this mixture in the microwave makes the water in the lemon juice turn to steam and evaporate, leaving behind lots of lemon flavor—and very little moisture. The result? Crunchy, flaky, lemony salt, speckled with bits of black pepper.

TRY IT THIS WAY!

EDAMAME WITH SRIRACHA-LIME SALT

Use **2 teaspoons grated lime zest** and **1 tablespoon lime juice** instead of lemon zest and juice. Use **1 tablespoon sriracha** instead of pepper.

CARAMELIZED ONION DIP

Yellow or Spanish onions work best in this recipe. Sweet or Vidalia onions will taste too sweet, and red onions will turn too dark in color. Serve with chips, crackers, or vegetables.

PREPARE INGREDIENTS

⅛ teaspoon baking soda

1 tablespoon plus ⅓ cup water, measured separately

2 onions (about 1 pound) peeled and sliced ¼ inch thick (see page 93) ▶

1 tablespoon vegetable oil

¼ teaspoon plus ½ teaspoon table salt, measured separately

1⅓ cups sour cream

2 tablespoons minced fresh chives

¾ teaspoon distilled white vinegar

⅛ teaspoon pepper

GATHER COOKING EQUIPMENT

2 bowls (1 medium, 1 small)

Spoon

10-inch nonstick skillet with lid

Oven mitts

Rubber spatula

Cutting board

Chef's knife

Plastic wrap

MAKES about 2 cups

TOTAL TIME 1 hour, plus chilling time

LEVEL ▪▪□

1. In small bowl, combine baking soda and 1 tablespoon water. Use spoon to stir until baking soda is dissolved, about 30 seconds. Set aside.

2. In 10-inch nonstick skillet, combine onions, oil, ¼ teaspoon salt, and remaining ⅓ cup water. Cook over medium-high heat until water is bubbling, about 2 minutes.

3. Cover skillet with lid and cook until water has mostly evaporated, about 5 minutes.

4. Use oven mitts to remove lid. Reduce heat to medium. Use rubber spatula to stir onions and gently press into bottom and sides of skillet. Cook, without stirring, for 1 minute.

5. Stir onions, scraping up browned bits from bottom and sides of skillet. Spread onions into even layer. Repeat gently pressing, cooking for 1 minute, and stirring until onions are softened, very brown, and look sticky, 12 to 15 minutes (see photo, right). (If onions look like they're burning instead of gently browning as they cook, turn heat down a bit.)

6. Add baking soda mixture to skillet and stir into onions. Cook, stirring constantly, until mixture has evaporated, about 30 seconds. Turn off heat.

7. Transfer onions to cutting board and let cool for 15 minutes. Use chef's knife to finely chop onions.

8. In medium bowl, combine sour cream, chives, vinegar, pepper, chopped onions, and remaining ½ teaspoon salt. Use rubber spatula to stir until well combined. Cover bowl with plastic wrap and place in refrigerator. Chill for at least 30 minutes and up to 24 hours. Serve.

BE WISE: CARAMELIZE!

All it takes to transform sharp-tasting raw onions into sweet and savory caramelized onions is a bit of chemistry. As the onions cook, two chemical reactions take place that create hundreds of new flavor and aroma compounds—and give the onions their brown color. Adding just a tiny bit of baking soda speeds up the process (and also makes the onions taste even sweeter!).

HOW TO CARAMELIZE ONIONS

Spread onions into even layer. Repeat gently pressing, cooking for 1 minute, and stirring until onions are softened, very brown, and look sticky, 12 to 15 minutes.

LOADED NACHOS

Serve these nachos with your favorite toppings, such as salsa, pickled jalapeños, chopped cilantro, diced avocado, and/or sour cream.

PREPARE INGREDIENTS

 1 teaspoon vegetable oil

 3 garlic cloves, peeled and minced (see page 94) ▶

1½ teaspoons chili powder

 ½ teaspoon ground cumin

 ¼ teaspoon dried oregano

 ¼ teaspoon table salt

 8 ounces 90 percent lean ground beef

 1 tablespoon tomato paste

 ½ teaspoon packed brown sugar

 ¼ cup water

 5 ounces (4 to 5 cups) tortilla chips

 ½ cup canned refried beans

1½ cups shredded Monterey Jack or Colby Jack cheese (6 ounces) (see page 13) ▶

GATHER COOKING EQUIPMENT

10-inch nonstick skillet

Wooden spoon

8-inch square baking dish

Spoon

Oven mitts

Cooling rack

SERVES 8

TOTAL TIME 45 minutes

LEVEL

1   Adjust oven rack to middle position and heat oven to 400 degrees.

2   In 10-inch nonstick skillet, heat oil over medium heat until shimmering, about 2 minutes (oil should be hot but not smoking; see page 11). ▶

3   Add garlic, chili powder, cumin, oregano, and salt and cook, stirring often with wooden spoon, until fragrant, about 30 seconds.

4   Add ground beef to skillet and cook, breaking up meat into small pieces with wooden spoon, until no longer pink, 2 to 4 minutes.

5   Stir in tomato paste and sugar and cook for 1 minute. Add water and cook until skillet is almost dry, 1 to 3 minutes. Turn off heat and slide skillet to cool burner.

6   Spread half of chips in even layer in 8-inch square baking dish. Use spoon to dollop half of refried beans over chips, then spoon half of beef mixture over beans (see photo, right). Sprinkle evenly with half of cheese. Repeat layering with remaining chips, beans, beef, and cheese.

7   Place baking dish in oven. Bake until cheese is melted and just beginning to brown, 9 to 11 minutes.

8   Use oven mitts to remove baking dish from oven and place on cooling rack (ask an adult for help). Let nachos cool for 2 minutes. Serve with your favorite toppings, if desired.

"NACHO" AVERAGE SNACK

The best nachos have a little bit of everything in every bite—crunchy chip, gooey cheese, beans, and beef. But to make that happen, you need to become a nacho engineer. First, create a solid base of crunchy tortilla chips. Then, add a layer of sturdy refried beans—they'll catch extra liquid from the seasoned ground beef and keep the chips below from getting too soggy. Next, a layer of shredded cheese that melts in the oven and helps the next layer (tortilla chips, again!) stick. Repeat, bake, snack!

Use spoon to dollop half of refried beans over chips, then spoon half of beef mixture over beans.

USING FRESH HERBS

Fresh herbs add lots of flavor and pops of color to all kinds of dishes. Learn about the most common herbs you'll use in this book, and how to prep them.

DELICATE HERBS

These herbs are usually added towards the end of a recipe, right before serving.

Basil

Delicate basil is very perishable! Don't buy too much at a time—the leaves shrivel and turn black in just a few days.

Parsley

There are two types of parsley: flat leaf (seen here) and curly leaf. Flat-leaf parsley has more flavor.

Mint

Mint makes your mouth feel cold when you eat it. You'll spot mint in both sweet and savory dishes.

Cilantro

Cilantro stems are tender and full of flavor—you can chop them up along with the leaves, if you like.

HEARTY HERBS

These sturdy herbs keep their flavor, even after they're cooked for a while—they're often added earlier in a recipe.

Rosemary

The taste of this woody herb reminds some people of pine trees (not flowers, despite having "rose" in its name).

Thyme

Thyme's tiny leaves pack a lot of flavor, so a little bit goes a long way.

HOW TO STORE, WASH, AND DRY FRESH HERBS

To Store

Wrap herbs in damp paper towels and place them in a zipper-lock plastic bag in the refrigerator. They will stay fresh for about a week. (Don't wash your herbs until right before starting the recipe.)

To Wash and Dry

The easiest way to wash fresh herbs is with a salad spinner. Fill the salad spinner bowl with cold water and add your fresh herbs. Gently swish the herbs around in the water. Lift the herbs out of the water and place them in the basket of the salad spinner. Discard water. Place the basket back into the salad spinner, place the lid on top, and spin the herbs dry.

HOW TO CHOP FRESH HERBS

1 Use your fingers to remove leaves from stems; discard stems.

2 Gather leaves in small pile. Place one hand on handle of chef's knife and rest fingers of your other hand on top of blade. Use rocking motion, pivoting knife as you chop.

VIDEO

 Chopping fresh herbs

CHEESY BREADSTICKS

You can use homemade or store-bought pizza dough for this recipe. If your pizza dough is cold from the fridge, you can leave it out on the counter for 1 to 2 hours to bring it to room temperature before starting.

PREPARE INGREDIENTS

1 pound pizza dough, room temperature

2 tablespoons unsalted butter, melted (see page 12) ▶

1½ teaspoons minced fresh thyme (see page 67) ▶

1½ teaspoons dried oregano

¾ teaspoon granulated garlic

¼ teaspoon kosher salt

¼ teaspoon pepper

½ cup shredded mozzarella cheese (2 ounces) (see page 13) ▶

¼ cup grated Parmesan cheese (½ ounce) (see page 13) ▶

GATHER COOKING EQUIPMENT

Rimmed baking sheet

Parchment paper

Chef's knife

Ruler

Pastry brush

Small bowl

Spoon

Oven mitts

Cooling rack

Spatula

Cutting board

SERVES 4 to 6

TOTAL TIME 50 minutes

LEVEL ◼◻◻

1   Adjust oven rack to middle position and heat oven to 450 degrees. Line rimmed baking sheet with parchment paper.

2   Place dough on clean counter. Use chef's knife to divide dough into 2 equal pieces. Shape dough following photo, right. Transfer both pieces of dough to parchment-lined baking sheet.

3   Use pastry brush to paint each dough piece evenly with melted butter. In small bowl, use spoon to stir thyme, oregano, granulated garlic, salt, and pepper until well combined. Sprinkle thyme mixture evenly over each dough piece. Sprinkle evenly with mozzarella and Parmesan.

4   Place baking sheet in oven. Bake until cheese is well browned and bubbling, 9 to 12 minutes.

5   Use oven mitts to remove baking sheet from oven and place on cooling rack (ask an adult for help). Let cool for 5 minutes.

6   Use spatula to carefully transfer cheesy bread to cutting board (baking sheet will be HOT!). Use chef's knife to cut each bread crosswise (the short way) into 8 breadsticks (there should be 16 total). Serve.

HOW TO SHAPE CHEESY BREADSTICKS

Use your hands to gently pat and stretch each piece of dough into 9-by-5-inch rectangle. Transfer both pieces of dough to parchment-lined baking sheet.

A CHEESY DYNAMIC DUO

A combination of mozzarella and Parmesan cheese make this the gooiest, cheesiest bread possible. Mozzarella is a great melter because it contains lots of water and its proteins (tiny molecules in the cheese) relax and spread out when the cheese heats up. Parmesan is an aged cheese (it sat in a special room for a year or more before it was sold). Lots of its water has already evaporated, which means Parmesan has a TON of flavor, but it's not so good at melting. Together, this duo gives our breadsticks the best of both cheesy worlds.

BAKED BRIE

You can use your favorite flavor of fruit preserves, such as strawberry, apricot, cherry, or mixed berry. Serve with sliced baguette or crackers.

PREPARE INGREDIENTS

1 (8-ounce) wheel Brie cheese

⅓ cup fruit preserves

¼ teaspoon chopped fresh thyme (see page 67) ▶

GATHER COOKING EQUIPMENT

1-quart baking dish

Spoon

Oven mitts

Cooling rack

SERVES 6

TOTAL TIME 40 minutes

LEVEL ▪■□

"This recipe was super easy and really good. Even my picky little brother liked it."
—Vivian, 11

START COOKING!

1 Adjust oven rack to middle position and heat oven to 350 degrees.

2 Place Brie in 1-quart baking dish. Use spoon to spread fruit preserves on top of Brie. Sprinkle with thyme.

3 Place baking dish in oven. Bake until cheese is very soft and cheese begins to bubble around edges, 17 to 20 minutes.

4 Use oven mitts to remove baking dish from oven and place on cooling rack (ask an adult for help). Let Brie cool for 5 minutes. Serve warm.

UN-"BRIE"-LIEVABLE CHEESE

Brie has a white rind on the outside and rich, creamy cheese on the inside. But, what is that rind . . . and can you eat it? Believe it or not, it's a totally edible (and delicious!) mold. When cheesemakers make Brie, they add a special mold that gives the cheese its mild flavor and buttery texture. That same mold also forms the rind, which protects the cheese inside from dangerous bacteria. When you bake Brie, the rind softens just enough so that you can easily scoop it up. "Brie" bold and eat this baked Brie with a cracker or slice of baguette, rind and all!

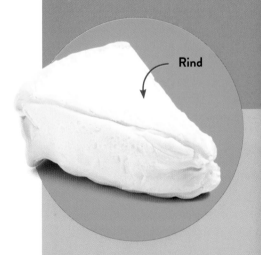

Rind

ROSEMARY SOCCA (CHICKPEA FLOUR PANCAKES)

You can top your socca with a drizzle of extra-virgin olive oil, grated Parmesan cheese, sautéed onions, and/or a pinch of flake sea salt.

PREPARE INGREDIENTS

¾ cup water

⅔ cup chickpea flour

½ teaspoon table salt

¼ teaspoon minced fresh rosemary (see page 67) ▶

Pinch ground cumin

2 tablespoons extra-virgin olive oil

GATHER COOKING EQUIPMENT

Medium bowl

Whisk

1-teaspoon measuring spoon

Liquid measuring cup

10-inch nonstick skillet

Spatula

Cutting board

Chef's knife

SERVES 2

TOTAL TIME 35 minutes

LEVEL ▪▪□□

"It was nice because it was soft but crunchy on the edges."
—Kai, 9

START COOKING!

1 In medium bowl, whisk water, chickpea flour, salt, rosemary, cumin, and 2 teaspoons oil until no lumps remain. Transfer batter to liquid measuring cup. Let sit for 10 minutes. (Batter will thicken as it sits.)

2 When batter is ready, add 2 teaspoons oil to 10-inch nonstick skillet. Heat over medium-high heat until just beginning to smoke, about 3 minutes. (You should start to see wisps of smoke coming up from oil—you may need to get eye level with pan to see this. Turn on your stove's vent hood if you have one; see page 11.) ▶

3 Swirl skillet to evenly coat with oil. Lift skillet off heat and pour half of batter (about ½ cup) into far side of skillet. Quickly swirl skillet in circles and shake until batter evenly covers bottom of skillet (see photos, right).

4 Return skillet to heat and cook socca until bottom is well browned and edges are crisp, 2 to 4 minutes (you can use spatula to loosen edges and peek at underside of socca to check).

5 Slide spatula under socca and flip. Cook until second side is light golden brown, 1 to 2 minutes. Carefully slide socca from skillet onto cutting board (use spatula to help transfer if needed).

6 Return skillet to heat and add remaining 2 teaspoons oil. Repeat cooking in steps 3 through 5 with remaining batter. Turn off heat.

7 Use chef's knife to cut socca into wedges. Serve.

HOW TO COOK SOCCA

1 Swirl skillet to evenly coat with oil. Lift skillet off heat and pour half of batter (about ½ cup) into far side of skillet.

2 Quickly swirl skillet in circles and shake until batter evenly covers bottom of skillet.

SUPERB SOCCA

While you may be familiar with the paper-thin, delicate French pancakes known as crepes, southeastern France has its own popular savory street-food pancake known as socca ("SOH-ka"). Also popular in Italy (where it's called farinata, torta di ceci, or cecina) socca are thin and crispy on the outside and soft and tender on the inside, with a slightly nutty flavor from the chickpea flour. Fun fact: Chickpea flour is simply ground-up dried chickpeas (also known as garbanzo beans), meaning that this dish is also gluten-free.

3 LUNCH

CHICKEN CAESAR SALAD WRAPS

Use a vegetable peeler to gently shave thin strips from the Parmesan cheese.

PREPARE INGREDIENTS

CAESAR DRESSING

- ½ cup mayonnaise
- ¼ cup grated Parmesan cheese (½ ounce) (see page 13) ▶
- ¼ cup extra-virgin olive oil
- 3 tablespoons lemon juice, squeezed from 1 lemon (see page 14) ▶
- 2 teaspoons Dijon mustard
- 2 teaspoons Worcestershire sauce
- 2 small garlic cloves, peeled and minced (see page 94) ▶
- 2 anchovy fillets, rinsed, patted dry, and minced (optional)
- ½ teaspoon table salt
- ¼ teaspoon pepper

WRAPS

- 1 cup shredded rotisserie or leftover chicken
- 2 (10-inch) flour tortillas
- 1 small romaine lettuce heart (about 4½ ounces), torn into bite-size pieces (about 3 cups)
- 1 tablespoon shaved Parmesan cheese

SERVES 2

TOTAL TIME 30 minutes

LEVEL

"I loved the flavor, and it made for a quick and easy meal!"
—Allegra, 13

GATHER COOKING EQUIPMENT

2 bowls
(1 medium, 1 small)

Whisk

Rubber spatula

1-tablespoon
measuring spoon

Cutting board

Chef's knife

START COOKING!

1   **For the Caesar dressing:** In small bowl, whisk all Caesar dressing ingredients until well combined.

2   **For the wraps:** In medium bowl, use rubber spatula to toss chicken with 2 tablespoons dressing until fully coated. Place tortillas on clean counter. Divide dressed chicken evenly between tortillas, arranging in center of each tortilla and leaving border around edge.

3   Add lettuce to now-empty bowl and toss with 2 tablespoons dressing until coated. Top chicken with dressed lettuce, dividing evenly between tortillas. Sprinkle shaved Parmesan evenly over lettuce.

4   Working with 1 tortilla at a time, roll tortillas into wraps following photos, above right.

5   Transfer wraps to cutting board, seam side down. Use chef's knife to cut wraps in half. Serve. (Remaining dressing can be refrigerated for up to 3 days.)

HOW TO ROLL UP A WRAP

1 Fold up bottom of tortilla over filling. Then fold in sides of tortilla over filling.

2 Working from bottom up, roll into log, ending with seam side down.

FISH IN SALAD DRESSING?

Anchovies are tiny fish that add lots of savory taste, called umami ("oo-MA-me"), to everything from sauces to stews to Caesar salad dressing. (Don't worry—they won't make your dressing taste fishy!) Umami is one of the five basic tastes, along with sweet, sour, salty, and bitter. The taste of umami can be described as meaty or savory. This Caesar dressing also includes two other umami-packed ingredients, Parmesan cheese and Worcestershire sauce, giving it even more savory goodness.

TURKEY AND CHEDDAR SANDWICHES WITH PICKLED APPLE

We like baby spinach on this sandwich, but you can use lettuce instead, if you prefer.

PREPARE INGREDIENTS

- 1 cup cider vinegar
- ½ cup sugar
- ½ teaspoon table salt
- 1 apple, cored and sliced thin (see photos, right)
- 2 tablespoons mayonnaise
- 2 teaspoons Dijon mustard
- 4 slices hearty multigrain or whole-wheat sandwich bread, toasted
- ½ cup baby spinach
- 2 slices deli cheddar cheese
- 4 slices deli turkey

GATHER COOKING EQUIPMENT

- 2 bowls (1 large microwave-safe, 1 small)
- Rubber spatula
- Oven mitts
- Colander
- Spoon
- Cutting board
- Chef's knife

SERVES 2

TOTAL TIME 35 minutes

LEVEL ■□□

"The pickled apple was weird and delicious!"
—Hayes, 12

1   In large microwave-safe bowl, use rubber spatula to stir together vinegar, sugar, and salt. Place bowl in microwave and heat until mixture is bubbling, about 3 minutes.

2   Use oven mitts to remove bowl from microwave (ask an adult for help). Add apple to bowl and stir until well combined. Let sit for 5 minutes.

3   Set colander in sink. Pour pickled apple into colander. Shake colander to drain well. Return pickled apple to now-empty bowl.

4   In small bowl, use spoon to stir together mayonnaise and mustard. Place toast on cutting board. Use back of spoon to spread mayonnaise mixture evenly over 1 side of each slice of toast.

5   Divide spinach, cheddar, and turkey evenly between 2 slices of toast. Place 4 to 6 slices pickled apple on top of turkey to cover. Top sandwiches with remaining slices of toast. Press down gently on each sandwich. Use chef's knife to cut sandwiches in half. Serve.

HOW TO CORE AND SLICE APPLES

1   Place apple on cutting board. Use chef's knife to slice around core to remove 4 large pieces.

2   Place apple pieces flat side down and slice thin.

IN A PICKLE

You've probably eaten pickled cucumbers, but you can actually turn just about any fruit or vegetable into a pickle! (Pickles are fruits or vegetables that have been preserved—treated so that they last longer before spoiling.) There are a few ways to make pickles, but the fastest is to soak the fruit or vegetable in an acidic liquid (in this recipe, we use vinegar). These quick-pickled apple slices provide crunchy, tangy contrast to the savory turkey and creamy cheese.

OPEN-FACED TUNA MELTS

You can use American or cheddar cheese in your tuna melts, or a combination!

PREPARE INGREDIENTS

1 (5-ounce) can solid white tuna in water, drained and flaked (see photo, right)

2 tablespoons mayonnaise

2 tablespoons finely chopped onion (see page 93)

2 tablespoons finely chopped celery

2 tablespoons chopped pickles

1 teaspoon Dijon mustard

1 teaspoon lemon juice, squeezed from ½ lemon (see page 14) ▶

¼ teaspoon pepper

Pinch table salt

2 slices hearty white sandwich bread

1 tablespoon unsalted butter, melted and cooled (see page 12) ▶

4 slices deli American cheese and/or deli cheddar cheese

GATHER COOKING EQUIPMENT

Rimmed baking sheet

Aluminum foil

Medium bowl

Spoon

Pastry brush

Oven mitts

Cooling rack

SERVES 2

TOTAL TIME 35 minutes

LEVEL ▪▪☐

START COOKING!

1 Adjust oven rack to middle position and heat oven to 450 degrees. Line rimmed baking sheet with aluminum foil.

2 In medium bowl, use spoon to mix tuna, mayonnaise, onion, celery, pickles, mustard, lemon juice, pepper, and salt until well combined.

3 Place bread slices on foil-lined baking sheet. Use pastry brush to paint melted butter evenly over 1 side of each slice of bread.

4 Flip each slice over (buttered side down). Divide tuna mixture evenly between slices of bread and use spoon to spread into even layer. Place 2 cheese slices on top of each sandwich.

5 Place baking sheet in oven. Bake until cheese is melted, 5 to 6 minutes.

6 Use oven mitts to remove baking sheet from oven and place on cooling rack (ask an adult for help). Let sandwiches cool slightly on baking sheet, about 2 minutes. Serve warm.

"CHEESE" YOUR OWN ADVENTURE

The star of this tuna melt is the cheesy "blanket" that tops each sandwich. American cheese transforms into gooey deliciousness in the oven, thanks to special salts that help it melt smoothly. But it doesn't have a whole lot of flavor. Enter: cheddar. Cheddar cheese doesn't contain those special salts, so it's not quite as gooey when it melts, but it IS full of flavor. For the best combo of flavor and meltiness, top your tuna with a slice of each!

HOW TO DRAIN AND FLAKE TUNA

Use can opener to open can of tuna. Drain tuna well over sink. Transfer tuna to bowl and use fork to flake tuna into small pieces.

KNIFE SAFETY

Knives might be the most important tools in your kitchen—you'll use one for everything from mincing herbs to chopping onions. Don't be intimidated! Sharpen your skills with these tips.

THE TWO ESSENTIAL KNIVES

A professional chef might have lots of different knives on hand, but for a home kitchen, these two knives are a cut above the rest.

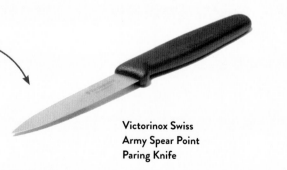

Opinel Le Petit Chef Cutlery Set (great for younger kids)

1 Chef's Knife

A chef's knife can help you tackle almost any task requiring knife work, such as mincing garlic, chopping peppers, or slicing chicken. Most chef's knife blades are about 8 inches long, but a chef's knife with a shorter blade (4 to 6 inches long) is easier for young chefs to handle—and will still do a great job.

Victorinox Swiss Army Fibrox Pro 6" Chef's Knife (great for older kids)

2 Paring Knife

This small knife is best suited for precision work, such as hulling strawberries or coring tomatoes. Its blade is usually about 3½ inches long and a little bit flexible.

Victorinox Swiss Army Spear Point Paring Knife

HOW TO HOLD A CHEF'S KNIFE

There are two important techniques that keep you safe and protect your fingertips while using a chef's knife.

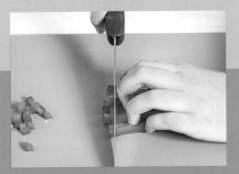

1 Always use "bear claw" grip to hold food in place and minimize danger: **Tuck in your fingertips, keeping them away from knife.** When you lift knife after making cut, reposition your "clawed" hand for next cut.

2 Rest your fingers on top of blade while mincing: **Grip knife handle with 1 hand, and rest fingers of other hand lightly on top of blade, away from tip.**

A SHARP KNIFE IS A SAFE KNIFE ▶

A dull knife is an accident waiting to happen because it's more likely to slip off food while you're using it. Here's how to tell if your knife is sharp.

With 1 hand, hold single piece of printer paper firmly at top. Using other hand, lay knife blade against top edge of paper at angle and slice away from you. If knife slices cleanly, it's sharp! If knife drags, ask an adult to help you sharpen knife with electric or manual sharpener.

VIDEO

▶ Testing knife sharpness

WEDGE SALADS WITH RANCH DRESSING

PREPARE INGREDIENTS

RANCH DRESSING

- ⅔ cup mayonnaise
- ⅓ cup buttermilk
- 2 tablespoons minced fresh cilantro (see page 67) ▶
- 2 tablespoons white wine vinegar
- ½ teaspoon onion powder
- ½ teaspoon garlic powder
- ½ teaspoon dried dill weed
- ⅛ teaspoon table salt
- ⅛ teaspoon pepper

SALADS

- 2 slices bacon
- ½ head (1 pound) iceberg lettuce
- 1 cup (6 ounces) cherry tomatoes, quartered
- 2 tablespoons crumbled blue cheese (optional)

GATHER COOKING EQUIPMENT

Medium bowl	Cutting board
Whisk	Chef's knife
Large microwave-safe plate	Serving plates
Paper towels	1-tablespoon measuring spoon
Oven mitts	

SERVES 4

TOTAL TIME 25 minutes

LEVEL ▪◻◻

1 **For the ranch dressing:** In medium bowl, whisk all ranch dressing ingredients until smooth.

2 **For the salads:** Line large microwave-safe plate with 2 paper towels and place bacon on top. Top with 2 more paper towels. Place plate in microwave and cook until bacon is crispy, 3 to 5 minutes.

3 Use oven mitts to remove plate from microwave (ask an adult for help). Set aside to cool.

4 Core and cut lettuce into wedges following photos, right.

5 Place 1 wedge of lettuce on each serving plate. Drizzle 2 tablespoons dressing over each wedge. Sprinkle with tomatoes and blue cheese (if using). Crumble and sprinkle half slice of bacon over each wedge.

6 Season salads with salt and pepper to taste (see page 58). Serve. (Remaining dressing can be refrigerated for up to 4 days.)

HOW TO CORE AND QUARTER ICEBERG LETTUCE

1 Place lettuce half on cutting board cut side up. Use chef's knife to cut out core from lettuce. Discard core.

2 Flip lettuce cut side down and cut into 4 equal wedges.

LIVING ON THE "WEDGE"

A wedge salad looks restaurant-worthy, with its bacon, tomatoes, and blue cheese piled atop a wedge of iceberg lettuce (yes, that's where the name "wedge salad" comes from). While the first printed wedge salad recipe appeared in 1916, it wasn't until the 1970s that the salad started popping up on steakhouse menus across the United States. This retro dish's best feature is how the mild-flavored lettuce acts as a blank canvas for those toppings and the tangy, creamy dressing. Grab a fork AND a knife and dig in!

PITA "PIZZAS" WITH HUMMUS, FETA, AND TOMATOES

PREPARE INGREDIENTS

- 2 (8-inch) pitas
- 2 teaspoons plus 2 teaspoons extra-virgin olive oil, measured separately
- 2 teaspoons red wine vinegar
- ⅛ teaspoon table salt
- ⅛ teaspoon pepper
- 6 cherry tomatoes, quartered
- 2 tablespoons chopped pitted kalamata olives
- ¼ cup hummus
- ½ cup shredded mozzarella cheese (2 ounces) (see page 13) ▶
- ½ cup crumbled feta cheese (2 ounces)
- 1 tablespoon chopped fresh parsley (optional) (see page 67) ▶

GATHER COOKING EQUIPMENT

- Pastry brush
- Rimmed baking sheet
- Oven mitts
- Cooling rack
- Medium bowl
- Rubber spatula
- Spatula
- Cutting board
- Chef's knife

SERVES 2

TOTAL TIME 1 hour

LEVEL ▪▪☐

START COOKING!

1   Adjust oven rack to middle position and heat oven to 450 degrees. Use pastry brush to paint bottoms of pitas with 2 teaspoons oil. Place pitas, oiled side down, on rimmed baking sheet.

2   Place baking sheet in oven. Bake until pitas are golden, about 5 minutes.

3   Use oven mitts to remove baking sheet from oven and place on cooling rack (ask an adult for help). Let cool for 10 minutes.

4   While pitas cool, in medium bowl, use rubber spatula to stir vinegar, salt, pepper, and remaining 2 teaspoons oil until combined. Add tomatoes and olives and stir until well coated.

5   When pitas have cooled, divide hummus evenly between pitas and use rubber spatula to spread into even layer.

6   Sprinkle mozzarella and feta evenly over hummus. Divide tomato mixture evenly over cheese.

7   Use oven mitts to place baking sheet in oven. Bake until pitas are golden brown around edges and mozzarella is melted, about 6 minutes.

8   Use oven mitts to remove baking sheet from oven and place on cooling rack (ask an adult for help). Let pizzas cool slightly on baking sheet, about 2 minutes. Use spatula to transfer pizzas to cutting board. Sprinkle pizzas with parsley (if using). Use chef's knife to cut pizzas into wedges. Serve.

PROTECT YOUR PITA

Pita makes a great base for these one-person "pizzas" that are inspired by the flavors of Greek salad—as long as it stays crisp! To avoid a soggy bottom, we brush the pitas with oil and bake them before adding the toppings— the oil helps the pitas get extra-crispy! Then, the layers of creamy hummus and melty cheese protect the pita from absorbing liquid from the juicy tomatoes and olives.

"The recipe was unique and tasty. I liked the blend of cheeses."
—Mallory, 10

CUCUMBER-AVOCADO MAKI

Do not substitute other short-grain rices for the sushi rice. If you can't find Persian cucumbers, use half an English cucumber, cut into eight spears. Serve the maki with soy sauce plus wasabi and pickled ginger, if desired.

PREPARE INGREDIENTS

- 1⅔ cups sushi rice
- 2 cups water
- ¾ teaspoon table salt
- 1½ tablespoons unseasoned rice vinegar
- 1½ teaspoons sugar
- 2 Persian cucumbers
- 4 (8-by-7½-inch) sheets nori
- 1 ripe avocado, halved, pitted, and sliced thin (see page 15) ▶
- Soy sauce

GATHER COOKING EQUIPMENT

- Fine-mesh strainer
- 2 bowls (1 large, 1 medium)
- Medium saucepan with lid
- Rubber spatula
- Oven mitts
- Cutting board
- Chef's knife
- Sushi mat or 10-inch square piece of parchment paper
- 1-cup dry measuring cup
- Ruler

SERVES 2 to 4 (Makes 4 rolls)

TOTAL TIME 1½ hours

LEVEL ■■□

"The cucumber and avocado complemented each other, giving a refreshing taste."
—Lulu, 13

START COOKING!

1. Set fine-mesh strainer over large bowl and set in sink. Place rice in strainer. Rinse rice under cold running water, emptying bowl a few times as it fills, until water in bowl is clear, 1½ to 2 minutes. Shake strainer to drain rice well. Discard water in bowl.

2. Transfer rice to medium saucepan. Use rubber spatula to stir in water and salt. Bring rice to boil over medium-high heat. Reduce heat to low, cover saucepan with lid, and cook for 20 minutes. Turn off heat and slide saucepan to cool burner. Let rice sit, covered, for 10 minutes to finish cooking.

3. Use oven mitts to remove lid. Use rubber spatula to transfer cooked rice to medium bowl (ask an adult for help). Stir vinegar and sugar into rice and let rice cool for 20 minutes.

4. While rice cools, place cucumbers on cutting board. Use chef's knife to trim ends of cucumbers and then discard ends. Cut cucumbers in half lengthwise (the long way). Lay cucumber halves flat side down and cut in half lengthwise again. (You should have 8 spears total.)

5. Fill and shape maki following photos, page 90. Transfer finished maki, seam side down, to clean cutting board. Repeat filling and shaping with remaining nori sheets, rice, avocado, and cucumber.

6. Use chef's knife to cut each maki crosswise (the short way) into 8 equal pieces (ask an adult for help). Serve with soy sauce for dipping.

KEEP GOING! →

SUSHI 101

Sushi, an iconic part of Japanese cuisine, traditionally includes cooked rice seasoned with vinegar, salt, and sugar. Sushi makers roll, fill, or top their rice with all sorts of ingredients, from superfresh raw fish to vegetables to shredded omelet. While there are many different types of sushi, some of the most popular are maki, temaki, and nigiri. In maki ("MAH-kee"), seasoned rice and nori (a sheet of dried seaweed) are rolled around a filling and then sliced into bite-size pieces. ("Maki" means "roll" in Japanese.) Temaki ("teh-MAH-kee") is made by rolling a cone of nori around seasoned rice and fillings. Nigiri ("knee-GEE-ree") doesn't use any nori; instead it features a pillow-shaped ball of seasoned rice that's usually topped with pieces of fresh raw fish.

1 Place 1 nori sheet, shiny side down, on sushi mat, with longer side parallel to bottom edge of mat.

2 Scoop 1 cup cooled rice onto nori. Lightly wet your hands and spread rice into even layer, all the way to edges except for 1-inch border at top.

3 Place one-fourth of avocado slices in line across middle of rice. Add 2 cucumber spears on top of avocado, overlapping ends slightly.

4 Use sushi mat to lift and roll bottom edge of nori sheet up and over vegetable filling.

5 Gently squeeze and pull mat toward you to tighten.

6 Lift up edge of mat and continue to roll remaining nori and rice into log. Use mat to gently squeeze outside to seal and tighten.

CHOPPING, SLICING, AND MINCING

Depending on the recipe, you might be asked to chop, slice, and/or mince ingredients, usually fruits and vegetables. (To learn how to mince fresh herbs, see page 67.)

VIDEOS

Slicing cucumbers

Chopping onions or shallots

Slicing onions

MEASURING UP		
Mince		⅛-inch pieces or smaller
Chop fine		⅛- to ¼-inch pieces
Chop		¼- to ½-inch pieces
Chop coarse		½- to ¾-inch pieces

HOW TO SLICE CUCUMBERS ▶

Place cucumber on cutting board. Use chef's knife to trim ends of cucumber (discard ends). Cut cucumber in half crosswise (the short way). Then cut each piece in half lengthwise (the long way). Lay pieces flat side down on cutting board and slice crosswise into thin half-moons.

HOW TO CHOP ONIONS OR SHALLOTS

Shallots are smaller, milder cousins of onions. If you're working with a small shallot, there's no need to cut it in half.

1 Cut onion in half through root end, then trim top of onion. Use your fingers to remove peel.

2 Place onion half flat side down. Starting 1 inch from root end, make several vertical cuts.

3 Rotate onion and slice across first cuts. As you slice, onion will fall apart into chopped pieces.

HOW TO SLICE ONIONS

Cut onion in half through root end (see photo 1, above). Trim both ends and discard. Use your fingers to remove peel. Place onion halves flat side down on cutting board. Slice onion vertically into thin strips (follow the grain—the long stripes on the onion).

KEEP GOING!

VIDEOS

Peeling and mincing garlic

Slicing and chopping bell peppers

HOW TO PEEL AND MINCE GARLIC

Garlic is sticky, so you may need to carefully wipe the pieces of garlic from the sides of the knife to get them back onto the cutting board, where you can cut them. You can also use a garlic press to both crush and mince garlic.

1 Crush clove with bottom of measuring cup to loosen papery skin. Use your fingers to remove and discard papery skin.

2 Place 1 hand on handle of chef's knife and rest fingers of your other hand on top of blade. Using rocking motion, chop garlic repeatedly into very small pieces, pivoting knife as you chop.

HOW TO SLICE AND CHOP BELL PEPPERS

1 Use chef's knife to slice off top and bottom of pepper. Remove and discard seeds and stem.

2 Slice down through side of pepper.

3 Press pepper so it lies flat on cutting board, skin side down. Slice pepper into strips.

4 Turn strips and cut crosswise (the short way) into pieces.

CREAMY SECRET INGREDIENT PASTA

You can substitute 6 ounces of any short pasta shape for the farfalle; however, the cup measurements will vary—use 2 cups of ziti, 2 cups of penne, or 2⅓ cups of medium shells.

PREPARE INGREDIENTS

1	quart water
2	large egg yolks (see page 37) ▶
¼	cup grated Parmesan cheese (½ ounce), plus extra for serving (see page 13) ▶
½	teaspoon garlic powder
¼	teaspoon mustard powder
2½	cups (6 ounces) farfalle pasta
¾	teaspoon table salt

GATHER COOKING EQUIPMENT

Colander

Large saucepan with lid

Medium bowl

Whisk

Wooden spoon

Ladle

Liquid measuring cup

1-tablespoon measuring spoon

SERVES 2

TOTAL TIME 35 minutes

LEVEL ◼◻

"It was very fun to make my own sauce with just a few ingredients."
—Emma, 13

1   Set colander in sink. In large saucepan, bring water to boil over high heat.

2   While water heats, in medium bowl, whisk egg yolks, Parmesan, garlic powder, and mustard powder until well combined.

3   Add pasta and salt to boiling water. Cook, stirring frequently with wooden spoon, until pasta is al dente (tender but still a bit chewy), 10 to 12 minutes. Turn off heat.

4   Use ladle to carefully transfer ¼ cup pasta cooking water to liquid measuring cup. Drain pasta in colander (ask an adult for help). Return drained pasta to now-empty saucepan.

5   Add 1 tablespoon reserved cooking water to egg yolk mixture and whisk until well combined. Repeat 2 more times with 2 more tablespoons reserved cooking water, whisking thoroughly after each addition.

6   Pour warm egg yolk mixture into saucepan with pasta. Use wooden spoon to stir constantly for 30 seconds. Cover saucepan with lid and let pasta sit for 1 minute.

7   Remove lid and stir pasta constantly again until sauce thoroughly coats pasta and is thickened, about 30 seconds. If needed, add remaining cooking water until sauce is loosened slightly and coats pasta well. Serve immediately with extra Parmesan.

THE SECRET INGREDIENT IS . . .

The egg yolks in this dish create a velvety sauce that coats each and every piece of pasta. Heat from the pasta cooks the yolks so that they're safe to eat, but you need to warm them up slowly or else they'll curdle and turn into scrambled eggs. How to do it? Add hot pasta cooking water to the egg yolks, a little bit at a time. This slowly raises the yolks' temperature, gently cooking them. This technique is called "tempering" and it also keeps the sauce smooth—save that scramble for breakfast!

KIMCHI-MISO RAMEN

PREPARE INGREDIENTS

1 tablespoon vegetable oil

3 scallions, root ends trimmed and scallions cut into 1-inch pieces

1 tablespoon white miso

2 teaspoons grated fresh ginger (see page 14) ▶

3 cups vegetable broth

1 cup water

½ cup cabbage kimchi, drained and chopped coarse

2 (3-ounce) packages ramen noodles, seasoning packets discarded

2 teaspoons soy sauce

Toppings (see "Make It Your Way!," right)

GATHER COOKING EQUIPMENT

Large saucepan

Wooden spoon

Ladle

Serving bowls

SERVES 2

TOTAL TIME 30 minutes

LEVEL ■■□

"The broth was perfect because you could taste each of the ingredients."
—Karina, 11

1   In large saucepan, heat oil over medium heat until shimmering, about 2 minutes (oil should be hot but not smoking; see page 11). (▶)

2   Add scallions and cook, stirring occasionally with wooden spoon, until scallions are browned and tender, about 2 minutes.

3   Stir in miso and ginger and cook, stirring constantly, for 30 seconds.

4   Add broth, water, and kimchi. Use wooden spoon to scrape up browned bits on bottom of saucepan. Bring mixture to boil.

5   Add noodles and cook, stirring occasionally to break up noodles, until tender, about 3 minutes. Turn off heat.

6   Stir in soy sauce. Ladle soup into serving bowls and add your favorite toppings. Serve.

FERMENTATION NATION

Dried ramen noodles are usually sold with a packet of salty (but not very flavorful) seasoning. To amp up the flavor in our ramen, we toss the packet and add two special ingredients instead: miso and kimchi. Miso ("MEE-so") is a salty, savory paste made from soybeans, and kimchi ("KIM-chee") is a spicy, crunchy Korean pickle that's most commonly made with napa cabbage. Both miso and kimchi are fermented ingredients—that means that bacteria and/or yeast have changed the soybeans' and cabbage's texture, smell, and flavor (in a good way!) and also prevented them from spoiling.

MAKE IT YOUR WAY!

Get creative with ramen toppings and take your soup to the next level! Some of our favorite additions are cooked corn kernels, thinly sliced scallions, bean sprouts, shredded nori, hard-cooked eggs, sriracha, chili crisp, and chili-garlic sauce.

SPICED RED LENTIL SOUP

PREPARE INGREDIENTS

- 1½ cups (10½ ounces) dried red lentils
- 2 tablespoons plus 3 tablespoons unsalted butter, measured separately
- 1 onion, peeled and chopped fine (see page 93)
- 1 teaspoon table salt
- 1 teaspoon ground coriander
- ½ teaspoon ground cumin
- ½ teaspoon pepper
- ¼ teaspoon ground ginger
- 1 tablespoon tomato paste
- 1 garlic clove, peeled and minced (see page 94) ▶
- 4 cups chicken broth
- 2 cups water
- 2 tablespoons lemon juice, squeezed from 1 lemon (see page 14) ▶
- 1½ teaspoons dried mint, crumbled
- 1 teaspoon paprika
- ¼ cup chopped fresh cilantro (see page 67) ▶

GATHER COOKING EQUIPMENT

Colander

Medium saucepan with lid

Wooden spoon

Whisk

Small microwave-safe bowl

Small microwave-safe plate

Oven mitts

Spoon

Ladle

Serving bowls

SERVES 4

TOTAL TIME 1 hour

LEVEL ■■□

1 Place colander in sink. Add lentils to colander. Search through lentils and pick out any small stones or broken lentils and discard. Rinse lentils under cold running water. Shake colander to drain.

2 In medium saucepan, melt 2 tablespoons butter over medium heat. Add onion and salt and cook, stirring occasionally with wooden spoon, until onion is softened, about 5 minutes.

3 Add coriander, cumin, pepper, and ginger and cook, stirring often, until fragrant, about 2 minutes. Stir in tomato paste and garlic and cook for 1 minute.

4 Stir in broth, water, and lentils and bring to simmer (small bubbles should break often across surface of mixture). Cook, stirring occasionally, until lentils are soft and about half are broken down, about 15 minutes.

5 Turn off heat and slide saucepan to cool burner. Add lemon juice. Whisk soup until lentils are mostly broken down, about 30 seconds (see photo, below right). Season with salt to taste (see page 58). Cover saucepan with lid to keep warm.

6 Place remaining 3 tablespoons butter in small microwave-safe bowl and cover with small microwave-safe plate. Heat in microwave at 50 percent power until melted, 30 to 60 seconds. Use oven mitts to remove bowl from microwave. Use spoon to stir in mint and paprika.

7 Use ladle to portion soup into serving bowls. Drizzle each bowl with spiced butter and sprinkle with cilantro. Serve.

IT'S THE "LENTIL" THINGS

Red lentils are the key to this soup's thick, slightly nubby texture. Usually you need a blender to make a pureed soup, but in this recipe a vigorous whisking does the trick. That's because red lentils, which don't have a skin, break down really easily—no skin means that they absorb water and soften quickly as they cook, in just about 15 minutes. (Fun fact: Red lentils are actually just split green or brown lentils with their skins removed!) About half the lentils break down as the soup simmers, and 30 seconds with a whisk takes care of breaking down the rest.

WHISK TO THICKEN LENTIL SOUP

Whisk soup until lentils are mostly broken down, about 30 seconds.

4 DINNER

PAN-SEARED CHICKEN BREASTS WITH GARLIC-HERB SAUCE

This may seem like a lot of salt for four chicken breasts—but don't worry, you're not eating it all! The salt is mixed with water to form a mixture called a brine, and only a tiny bit is absorbed by the chicken.

PREPARE INGREDIENTS

- 2 quarts water
- ½ cup table salt for brining
- 4 (6- to 8-ounce) boneless, skinless chicken breasts
- ¼ teaspoon pepper
- 1 tablespoon extra-virgin olive oil
- 1 shallot, peeled and minced (see page 93)
- 2 garlic cloves, peeled and minced (see page 94) ▶
- ¾ cup chicken broth
- ½ teaspoon minced fresh thyme (see page 67) ▶
- ½ teaspoon white wine vinegar
- 4 tablespoons unsalted butter, cut into 4 pieces and chilled

GATHER COOKING EQUIPMENT

Large bowl	Tongs
Whisk	Instant-read thermometer
Large plate	
Paper towels	Serving platter
12-inch nonstick skillet	Aluminum foil
	Wooden spoon

SERVES 4

TOTAL TIME 45 minutes, plus brining time

LEVEL ◼◻◻

"I liked how the brine kept the chicken moist."
—Cara, 12

START COOKING!

1 In large bowl, whisk water and salt until salt dissolves. Place chicken in brine. Wash your hands. Place bowl in refrigerator and chill for 30 minutes.

2 Line large plate with paper towels. Remove chicken from brine and place on paper towel–lined plate. Discard brine. Use more paper towels to pat chicken dry. Sprinkle pepper evenly over all 4 chicken breasts. Wash your hands.

3 In 12-inch nonstick skillet, heat oil over medium heat until shimmering, about 2 minutes (oil should be hot but not smoking; see page 11). ▶

4 Use tongs to carefully place chicken in skillet. Cook until browned on first side, 6 to 8 minutes.

5 Use clean tongs to flip chicken. Cook until chicken registers 165 degrees on instant-read thermometer (see page 113), 6 to 10 minutes (ask an adult for help). Turn off heat. ▶

6 Use clean tongs to transfer chicken to serving platter. Cover loosely with aluminum foil.

7 Add shallot and garlic to now-empty skillet. Cook over medium heat, stirring constantly with wooden spoon, until softened, about 1 minute.

8 Add broth and use wooden spoon to scrape up any browned bits on bottom of skillet. Cook for 5 minutes. Turn off heat.

9 Stir in thyme and vinegar. Stir in chilled butter, 1 piece at a time, until butter is melted and sauce is well combined. Spoon sauce over chicken. Serve.

TIME TO BRINE

Chicken breasts don't contain much fat—that means they can taste bland and dry when you cook them. But juicy, perfectly seasoned chicken can be yours, all thanks to the power of the brine. A brine is a solution made of salt and water. As the raw chicken sits in the brine, some of the salt makes its way into the chicken due to a process called diffusion ("di-FEW-shun"). During diffusion, salt travels from the brine, where there's lots of it, into the chicken, where there's less of it, seasoning the chicken all the way through. At the same time, water travels from the brine into the chicken through a process called osmosis ("oz-MOE-sis"), making it juicier. The salt helps in the juiciness department, too—when it travels into the chicken, it changes the shape of the chicken's proteins, allowing the meat to hold on to more water and also keeping it tender.

OVEN-BAKED CHICKEN WITH TERIYAKI SAUCE

You can find mirin, a sweet rice wine, in the Japanese section of many supermarkets or in Japanese markets. Serve this dish with white rice.

PREPARE INGREDIENTS

½ cup soy sauce

¼ cup sugar

1 tablespoon mirin

1 (1-inch) piece ginger, peeled and sliced crosswise (the short way) (see page 14)

3 garlic cloves, peeled (see page 94)

1½ pounds boneless, skinless chicken thighs

GATHER COOKING EQUIPMENT

Small microwave-safe bowl

Oven mitts

Spoon

Liquid measuring cup

Blender

Dish towel

Large zipper-lock plastic bag

Rimmed baking sheet

Aluminum foil

2 cooling racks

Tongs

Cutting board

Chef's knife

Serving platter

SERVES 4

TOTAL TIME 1¼ hours, plus 1¼ hours cooling and chilling time

LEVEL ■■☐

"This is one of the best recipes I have tested. I marinated the chicken overnight, and it was so good."
—Aidan, 12

START COOKING!

1. In small microwave-safe bowl, combine soy sauce, sugar, and mirin. Heat in microwave until bubbling, about 2 minutes. Use oven mitts to remove from microwave. Use spoon to stir until sugar is dissolved. Let cool completely, about 20 minutes.

2. Measure ¼ cup cooled teriyaki sauce into liquid measuring cup. Pour remaining sauce into blender jar. Add ginger and garlic. Place lid on top of blender and hold lid firmly in place with folded dish towel. Turn on blender and process mixture until smooth, about 30 seconds. Stop blender.

3. Place chicken in large zipper-lock plastic bag. Wash your hands. Pour mixture from blender into bag. Press out air, seal bag, and turn to coat chicken. Refrigerate for at least 1 hour or up to 24 hours.

4. Adjust oven rack to upper-middle position and heat oven to 450 degrees. Line rimmed baking sheet with aluminum foil. Set 1 cooling rack in baking sheet.

5. Use tongs to remove chicken from bag and place on cooling rack set in baking sheet.

6. Place baking sheet in oven and bake until chicken begins to brown on top, about 20 minutes.

7. Use oven mitts to remove baking sheet from oven and place on second cooling rack (ask an adult for help). Use clean tongs to flip chicken.

8. Continue to bake until chicken is well browned and beginning to char in spots, 10 to 15 minutes.

9. Use oven mitts to remove baking sheet from oven and place on cooling rack. Let chicken cool for 5 minutes.

10. Use clean tongs to transfer chicken to cutting board. Use chef's knife to cut chicken crosswise (the short way) into ½-inch strips (see photo, above right). Transfer sliced chicken to serving platter. Drizzle with reserved ¼ cup teriyaki sauce. Serve.

HOW TO SLICE CHICKEN THIGHS

Use chef's knife to cut chicken crosswise (the short way) into ½-inch strips.

TERRIFIC TERIYAKI

In Japanese, the word "teriyaki" roughly translates as "shiny grilled." Traditional teriyaki is made by marinating meat in a sweet-and-salty sauce and then grilling or broiling it to make the surface turn shiny and slightly charred. In this recipe, we moved the chicken from the grill to the oven, making things a little safer while still creating juicy meat with crispy, caramelized edges. The simple sauce in this recipe is based on Chef Toshi Kasahara's version of traditional Japanese chicken teriyaki, which he serves at Toshi's Teriyaki Grill in Mill Creek, Washington. It's thinner than some American versions of teriyaki, but full of bold flavors.

AVGOLEMONO SOUP
(GREEK CHICKEN AND RICE SOUP WITH EGG AND LEMON)

PREPARE INGREDIENTS

3 (6-ounce) boneless, skinless chicken breasts, each cut into 3 pieces lengthwise (the long way)

1½ teaspoons table salt

8 cups chicken broth

1 cup long-grain white rice

1 tablespoon grated lemon zest plus ¼ cup juice, zested and squeezed from 2 lemons (see page 14)

1 garlic clove, peeled and minced (see page 94)

1 teaspoon ground coriander

¼ teaspoon pepper

2 large eggs plus 2 large egg yolks (see page 37)

2 teaspoons chopped fresh dill (see page 67)

GATHER COOKING EQUIPMENT

Medium bowl	2 forks
Tongs	Ladle
Large saucepan with lid	Liquid measuring cup
Oven mitts	Blender
Instant-read thermometer	Dish towel
Large plate	Wooden spoon

SERVES 4 to 6

TOTAL TIME 1¼ hours

LEVEL ▪▫▫

"It's 'dill'-icious. I loved all the flavors, especially the lemon!"
—Bethany, 11

1   In medium bowl, combine chicken and salt, and use
    tongs to toss chicken until coated. Let sit at room
    temperature for at least 15 minutes or up to 30 minutes.

2   In large saucepan, combine broth, rice, lemon zest,
    garlic, coriander, and pepper. Bring mixture to boil over
    high heat. Reduce heat to low, cover with lid, and cook
    for 5 minutes.

3   Use oven mitts to remove lid. Use tongs to add chicken
    to saucepan. Cover with lid and cook for 2 minutes. Turn
    off heat.

4   Let sit, covered, until rice is tender and chicken registers
    165 degrees on instant-read thermometer (see page 113),
    about 15 minutes (ask an adult for help). ▶

5   Use oven mitts to remove lid. Use clean tongs to transfer
    chicken to large plate and let cool slightly. Use 2 forks
    to shred chicken into bite-size pieces (see photo,
    below right).

6   Use ladle to carefully measure out 1 cup cooked rice
    into liquid measuring cup (leaving as much liquid
    behind in saucepan as possible—ask an adult for help).
    Pour into blender jar. Add lemon juice and eggs and
    egg yolks.

7   Place lid on top of blender and hold lid firmly in place
    with folded dish towel. Turn on blender and process
    mixture until smooth, about 1 minute.

8   Return shredded chicken and any juices to saucepan.
    Bring soup to simmer over high heat (small bubbles
    should break often across surface of mixture). Turn off
    heat and slide saucepan to cool burner.

9   Use wooden spoon to stir in blended rice mixture
    and dill. Season with salt and pepper to taste (see
    page 58). Serve.

SMOOCH YOUR SOUP

Avgolemono ("ahv-go-LEH-mo-no") soup gets its thick, creamy texture from eggs and rice. As they heat up, proteins (tiny molecules) in the eggs unfurl and become tangled, trapping some of the soup's water. Blending a cup of the cooked rice releases starch (another kind of molecule) that thickens the soup by trapping even more water. To be extra-sure that your soup stays smooth, follow Greek tradition and make a kissing sound and chant the "avgolemono prayer" ("please don't curdle, please don't curdle!") as you add the egg mixture.

HOW TO SHRED CHICKEN

Use 2 forks to pull cooked chicken apart into bite-size pieces.

SLOW-ROASTED SALMON

This recipe was developed with farmed salmon. If using wild salmon, cook the salmon to 120 degrees and reduce the cooking time in step 3 to 30 to 40 minutes. You might see small white clumps appear on the salmon as it cooks—this is normal! It's albumin ("al-BUE-min"), a protein found in salmon that clumps when it heats up. You can scrape it off before serving, if desired.

PREPARE INGREDIENTS

- 2 teaspoons packed brown sugar
- ¼ teaspoon pepper
- ¾ teaspoon plus ½ teaspoon kosher salt, measured separately
- 1 (2-pound) skinless salmon fillet, about 1 inch thick
- ¼ cup extra-virgin olive oil
- 1 tablespoon minced fresh parsley, mint, or basil (see page 67) (▶)
- 1 teaspoon grated lime zest plus 1 tablespoon juice, zested and squeezed from ½ lime (see page 14) (▶)

GATHER COOKING EQUIPMENT

2 small bowls

Spoon

13-by-9-inch baking dish

Instant-read thermometer

Oven mitts

Cooling rack

Chef's knife

SERVES 4 to 6

TOTAL TIME 1¼ hours

LEVEL ◼◻◻

"It was perfectly cooked, and the sauce gave it an extra burst of flavor!"
—Verona, 9

1 Adjust oven rack to middle position and heat oven to 250 degrees. In 1 small bowl, use spoon to mix brown sugar, pepper, and ¾ teaspoon salt.

2 Sprinkle brown sugar mixture on both sides of salmon. Place salmon, skinned side down, in 13-by-9-inch baking dish. (The skinned side of a skinless salmon fillet has a slightly darker color and a streaky appearance.) Wash your hands.

3 Place baking dish in oven. Roast until center of salmon fillet registers 125 degrees on instant-read thermometer (see page 113), 50 minutes to 1 hour (ask an adult for help). ▶

4 Meanwhile, in second small bowl, use clean spoon to stir oil, parsley, lime zest and juice, and remaining ½ teaspoon salt until combined.

5 When salmon is ready, use oven mitts to remove baking dish from oven and place on cooling rack (ask an adult for help).

6 Immediately pour oil mixture evenly over salmon. Let salmon sit for 5 minutes. Use chef's knife to cut salmon into pieces. Serve.

TAKE IT SLOW

Cooking salmon slowly in the oven at a (relatively) low temperature gives you moist, ultratender fish—and an impressive main dish for dinner. This gentle roasting technique lets the salmon cook all the way through while preventing the outside from getting too hot and turning tough. Bonus: There's none of the messy splattering that can happen when you're cooking at a higher temperature.

TWO TYPES OF SALMON

You might see salmon labeled "wild" and "farmed" at the grocery store. Wild salmon are caught by fisherfolk in open waters, usually in the northern Pacific Ocean. Farmed salmon, usually a species called Atlantic salmon, are bred and raised in aquaculture systems, which are like ocean farms. (Today, most Atlantic salmon is farmed due to overfishing in the 1900s.) Farmed salmon has more fat than wild salmon, giving it a richer texture. It can also be cooked to a slightly higher temperature (125 degrees versus 120 degrees for wild salmon) and still stay moist.

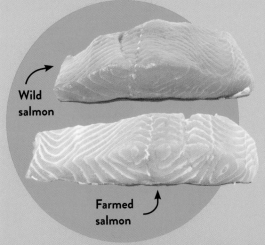

Wild salmon

Farmed salmon

COOKING PROTEINS

Knowing the right way to prep and cook animal proteins—chicken, turkey, beef, pork, and fish—is a key kitchen skill. Here, you'll learn the essential protein-cooking techniques.

PROTEIN SAFETY 101

Raw protein can contain harmful bacteria. To cook chicken, turkey, beef, pork, or fish safely, always follow these rules.

Wash your hands with hot, soapy water after handling raw protein or eggs. Also, wash any counters or cutting boards that came into contact with them.

Don't let raw protein; its juices; raw eggs; or your unwashed hands touch foods that you will eat raw, such as salad greens.

IT'S ALL IN THE PREP

Pat Your Protein Dry

In cooking, moisture is the enemy of browning—and browned food is delicious! When browning is the goal, patting raw chicken, turkey, beef, pork, or fish dry before cooking not only helps it brown in the pan but also helps reduce messy splattering on the stovetop.

Season It

There are two ways to season a protein: Sprinkle it with salt (see "Salt High," page 58) and/or pepper, or let it sit in a brine (a mixture of salt and water—see "Time to Brine," page 105). For lean proteins, such as chicken breasts, brining not only seasons the meat inside and out but also helps keep it juicy.

HOW TO TELL WHEN PROTEINS ARE DONE ▶

The most accurate way to check if a protein is fully cooked is to use an instant-read thermometer.

To check the temperature, insert the tip of the thermometer into the center of the thickest part of the food, making sure to avoid any bones. You can use tongs to lift individual pieces and then insert the thermometer sideways into the food.

GIVE IT A REST

Letting protein (except for delicate fish) rest once it's cooked allows it to reabsorb some of its juices. If you cut it right away, those juices will end up on your cutting board, not in your food!

VIDEO

 Temping proteins

FISH TACOS WITH CREAMY CILANTRO SAUCE

You can substitute halibut or haddock for the cod, if desired. Serve with your favorite taco toppings, such as chopped avocado or tomatoes, pickled onions, lime wedges, and/or hot sauce.

PREPARE INGREDIENTS

SLAW AND SAUCE

3 cups (8¼ ounces) coleslaw mix

¼ teaspoon grated lime zest, plus 2 tablespoons juice, zested and squeezed from 1 lime (see page 14) ▶

¼ teaspoon plus ¼ teaspoon table salt, measured separately

¼ cup sour cream

¼ cup mayonnaise

2 tablespoons milk

1 tablespoon chopped fresh cilantro (see page 67) ▶

FISH TACOS

2 teaspoons vegetable oil

1 teaspoon ground coriander

½ teaspoon ground cumin

¼ teaspoon chili powder

½ teaspoon table salt

2 (6- to 8-ounce) skinless cod fillets, 1 to 1½ inches thick

8–10 (6-inch) corn tortillas

SERVES 4 (Makes 8 to 10 tacos)

TOTAL TIME 50 minutes

LEVEL ■■□

> *"The sauce was creamy, the coleslaw was crunchy, and the seasoning for the fish tasted like it came from a restaurant."*
> —Reagan, 9

GATHER COOKING EQUIPMENT

3 bowls
(1 large, 2 small)

Rubber spatula

1-tablespoon
measuring spoon

Pastry brush

10-inch
nonstick skillet

Spoon

2 plates
(1 large, 1 small
microwave-safe)

Paper towels

Tongs

Spatula

Instant-read
thermometer

2 forks

Dish towel

FLAKING OUT

Cooked fish, such as cod, easily flakes into bite-size pieces—so easily, in fact, that you barely need to touch it before it falls apart. Why is fish so flaky? It comes down to its structure. Fish is made of thin layers of muscle fibers (supertiny strands, thinner than even a strand of hair) surrounded by very thin layers of connective tissue. When you flake cooked fish, it easily falls apart into those thin layers. Other meat, such as chicken or beef, has thicker bunches of muscle fibers surrounded by connective tissue—you can shred it into small pieces, but it won't "flake" the way that fish does.

1 **For the slaw and sauce:** In large bowl, use rubber spatula to stir coleslaw mix, 1 tablespoon lime juice, and ¼ teaspoon salt until combined.

2 In small bowl, use rubber spatula to stir sour cream, mayonnaise, milk, cilantro, lime zest, remaining 1 tablespoon lime juice, and remaining ¼ teaspoon salt until combined.

3 **For the fish tacos:** Use pastry brush to paint 10-inch nonstick skillet with oil. In second small bowl, use spoon to stir coriander, cumin, chili powder, and ½ teaspoon salt until well combined.

4 Place cod on large plate. Use paper towels to pat cod dry. Sprinkle coriander mixture evenly on all sides of cod. Place cod in oiled skillet. Wash your hands.

5 Place skillet over medium heat and cook for 6 minutes. Use tongs and spatula to carefully flip cod.

6 Continue to cook until center of cod registers 140 degrees on instant-read thermometer (see page 113), 4 to 8 minutes (ask an adult for help). Turn off heat and slide skillet to cool burner. ▶

7 Transfer cod to clean large plate. Use 2 forks to flake cod into pieces.

8 Stack tortillas on small microwave-safe plate and cover with damp dish towel. Heat in microwave until warm, about 1 minute.

9 Divide cod evenly among warmed tortillas. Top with slaw and drizzle with sauce. Serve with your favorite toppings.

HONEY-MUSTARD PORK CHOPS

For the best results, be sure to use pork chops of a similar size so that they cook evenly.

PREPARE INGREDIENTS

Vegetable oil spray

2 tablespoons unsalted butter

½ cup panko bread crumbs

3 tablespoons yellow mustard

2 tablespoons honey

1 tablespoon mayonnaise

2 teaspoons packed brown sugar

1 teaspoon table salt

1 garlic clove, peeled and minced (see page 94) ▶

½ teaspoon pepper

½ teaspoon paprika

4 (6- to 8-ounce) boneless pork chops, ¾ to 1 inch thick

GATHER COOKING EQUIPMENT

Rimmed baking sheet

Aluminum foil

2 cooling racks

10-inch skillet

Rubber spatula

2 small bowls

Spoon

Paper towels

Pastry brush

1-tablespoon measuring spoon

Instant-read thermometer

Oven mitts

SERVES 4

TOTAL TIME 1½ hours

LEVEL ■■□

START COOKING!

1 Adjust oven rack to middle position and heat oven to 275 degrees. Line rimmed baking sheet with aluminum foil and set 1 cooling rack in baking sheet. Spray cooling rack with vegetable oil spray.

2 In 10-inch skillet, melt butter over medium heat. Add panko and cook, stirring often with rubber spatula, until lightly browned, 3 to 5 minutes. Turn off heat. Transfer toasted panko to small bowl and let cool for 10 minutes.

3 Meanwhile, in second small bowl, use spoon to stir mustard, honey, mayonnaise, brown sugar, salt, garlic, pepper, and paprika until well combined.

4 Use paper towels to pat pork chops dry. Place pork chops on greased rack in baking sheet, leaving space between chops.

5 Use pastry brush to paint mustard mixture over top and sides of each pork chop (leave bottoms uncoated). Top with toasted panko following photo, below right. Wash your hands.

6 Place baking sheet in oven and bake until pork registers 140 degrees on instant-read thermometer (see page 113), 50 minutes to 1 hour (ask an adult for help). ▶

7 Use oven mitts to remove baking sheet from oven and place on second cooling rack (ask an adult for help). Let pork chops rest for 10 minutes. Serve.

LOW AND SLOW

To keep as much moisture as possible in pork chops, lots of recipes cook them quickly in a hot skillet. But there's another way! We bake these pork chops at a low temperature for a long time, similar to how you'd cook a fattier cut, such as pork shoulder. This keeps the chops' temperature low so that the outsides don't overcook and turn tough before the interiors finish cooking. Plus, low heat also helps special molecules, called enzymes ("EN-zimes"), break down some of the pork's proteins, creating more tender meat. Chewy chops no more!

HOW TO COAT PORK CHOPS

Scoop 2 tablespoons toasted panko onto each pork chop. Spread panko into even layer and press lightly to stick.

SIZZLING BEEF LETTUCE WRAPS

Start by making the Quick Pickled Cucumbers (see below right). They can sit in the brine while you make the rest of this recipe. If you like things spicy, use the full amount of sriracha.

PREPARE INGREDIENTS

1 recipe Quick Pickled Cucumbers (see right)

¼ cup mayonnaise

1–2 teaspoons sriracha

3 tablespoons soy sauce

2 tablespoons packed brown sugar

4 garlic cloves, peeled and minced (see page 94)

1 tablespoon toasted sesame oil

1 pound 85 percent lean ground beef

2 tablespoons water

¼ teaspoon baking soda

1 head Bibb lettuce (8 ounces), leaves separated

½ cup fresh cilantro leaves

4 scallions, dark-green parts only, sliced thin

GATHER COOKING EQUIPMENT

3 bowls (1 medium, 2 small)

Spoon

Wooden spoon

12-inch nonstick skillet

Serving platter

3 small serving bowls

SERVES 4

TOTAL TIME 1 hour, plus time to make Quick Pickled Cucumbers

LEVEL ■■□

"The flavors were very vivid! I loved the taste of the toasted sesame oil in the ground beef."
—Anya, 13

START COOKING!

1 In small bowl, use spoon to stir mayonnaise and sriracha until well combined; set aside.

2 In second small bowl, combine soy sauce, brown sugar, garlic, and oil.

3 In medium bowl, use wooden spoon to mix beef, water, and baking soda until well combined. Let beef sit at room temperature for 5 minutes.

4 Add beef mixture to 12-inch nonstick skillet. Cook over medium-high heat, breaking up meat into small pieces with wooden spoon, until no longer pink, 8 to 10 minutes.

5 Carefully add soy sauce mixture to skillet (sauce will bubble up) and stir to combine (ask an adult for help). Cook until most of liquid evaporates, 3 to 4 minutes. Turn off heat.

6 Carefully transfer beef to 1 side of serving platter (ask an adult for help). Arrange lettuce leaves on other side of platter.

7 Place pickled cucumbers, cilantro, and scallions in individual serving bowls. To serve, fill lettuce leaves with beef mixture and top with pickled cucumbers, cilantro, scallions, and sriracha mayonnaise.

TRY A LITTLE TENDERNESS

For ground beef that's moist and tender instead of tough, we turn to an ingredient that's more common in cookie and cake recipes: baking soda. Mixing the raw ground beef with baking soda changes the meat's pH (how acidic it is), making it harder for proteins to link up as the beef cooks. (Too many linked-up proteins create tough meat.) The result: a tender filling that's a perfect match for crunchy lettuce, tangy pickles, and a spicy sauce.

QUICK PICKLED CUCUMBERS

In medium microwave-safe bowl, combine 1 cup unseasoned rice vinegar, 3 tablespoons sugar, and ½ teaspoon table salt. Heat in microwave until hot and beginning to bubble at edges, 1 to 2 minutes. Use oven mitts to remove bowl from microwave (ask an adult for help). Stir mixture with spoon until sugar dissolves. Add 4 Persian cucumbers, trimmed and sliced into half-moons (see page 92). Let mixture sit, stirring occasionally, for 45 minutes. Use slotted spoon to serve pickles. (Pickles can be refrigerated in brine for up to 1 week.) ▶

COOKING PASTA

Learn how to cook "pasta"-tively perfect noodles, every time, with the information, tips, and tricks on these pages.

USE THE RIGHT RATIO

When you cook pasta in a large pot of boiling water, such as in Pasta with Kale-Basil Pesto (page 124), adding salt to the boiling water seasons the pasta inside and out. The right ratio of pasta to water to salt helps make sure that your pasta is perfectly seasoned.

PASTA	WATER	SALT
1 pound	4 quarts	1 tablespoon table salt
¾ pound (12 ounces)	4 quarts	1 tablespoon table salt
½ pound (8 ounces)	2 quarts	1½ teaspoons table salt

HOW TO TELL WHEN PASTA IS DONE

Lots of recipes tell you to cook pasta until it is al dente ("al DEN-tay"), which means "to the tooth" in Italian. That means the pasta is still a bit firm when you bite into it. If you cook pasta too long, it turns mushy. The best way to tell if pasta is al dente? Take a bite!

Use a wooden spoon to scoop out one piece of pasta and transfer it to a colander in the sink. Run the pasta under cold water for a few seconds and then taste it. If the pasta feels hard and a little dry, keep cooking for another few minutes. If the pasta is mostly tender but still firm at the center, it's done! For thicker pasta shapes, such as rigatoni or tagliatelle, take a bite and then look at the cross section of the pasta. If it's mostly yellow with a tiny strip of white at the center, it's probably al dente.

Save Some Pasta Water

Many recipes tell you to reserve some of the pasta cooking water before you drain the noodles and then add it when you're combining the pasta and sauce. The cooking water contains starch from the pasta, which helps the sauce coat each and every noodle.

ANOTHER WAY TO COOK PASTA

Two of the recipes in this book—Oven-Baked Spaghetti and Meatballs (page 122) and One-Pot Garlicky Shrimp Pasta (page 126)—cook pasta right in a measured amount of sauce instead of in a separate pot of boiling water. As it cooks, the pasta absorbs some of the sauce, giving it an extra boost of flavor. Bonus: no extra pot or colander to wash!

OVEN-BAKED SPAGHETTI AND MEATBALLS

You can substitute plant-based beef for the ground beef—our favorite is from Impossible Foods.

PREPARE INGREDIENTS

Vegetable oil spray

½ cup panko bread crumbs

½ cup milk

12 ounces spaghetti

1 (24-ounce) jar marinara sauce

2 cups water, plus extra hot water as needed

1 pound 85 percent lean ground beef

½ cup grated Parmesan cheese (1 ounce), plus extra for serving (see page 13) ▶

½ teaspoon garlic powder

½ teaspoon dried oregano

½ teaspoon table salt

2 tablespoons torn fresh basil

GATHER COOKING EQUIPMENT

13-by-9-inch baking dish	1-tablespoon measuring spoon
Large bowl	Aluminum foil
Rubber spatula	Oven mitts
Tongs	Cooling rack

SERVES 4

TOTAL TIME 1¼ hours

LEVEL ▪◻◻

"It was a fun technique to cook everything all together. Everyone in my family liked it!"
—Emma, 13

START COOKING!

1 Adjust oven rack to middle position and heat oven to 475 degrees. Spray 13-by-9-inch baking dish with vegetable oil spray.

2 In large bowl, use rubber spatula to combine panko and milk. Let mixture sit for 5 minutes.

3 Meanwhile, use your hands to break pasta in half over greased baking dish. Spread pasta into even layer. Pour marinara sauce and water over pasta and use tongs to toss gently until coated.

4 Add beef, Parmesan, garlic powder, oregano, and salt to bowl with panko mixture and use your hands to gently mix until evenly combined.

5 Roll beef mixture into 15 meatballs (about 2 tablespoons each). Place meatballs in baking dish on top of pasta. Wash your hands.

6 Cover baking dish tightly with aluminum foil. Place baking dish in oven and bake for 30 minutes.

7 Use oven mitts to remove baking dish from oven and place on cooling rack (ask an adult for help). Carefully remove foil and discard. Use tongs to stir pasta thoroughly, scraping sides and bottom of dish (be careful—baking dish and sauce will be HOT!).

8 Return baking dish to oven and continue to bake, uncovered, until pasta is tender and sauce is thickened, 5 to 8 minutes.

9 Ask an adult to remove baking dish from oven and place on cooling rack. Let pasta cool for 10 minutes.

10 Use tongs to carefully toss to coat pasta and meatballs with sauce. (If sauce is too thick, add extra hot water, 1 tablespoon at a time, until loosened.) Sprinkle with basil and serve with extra Parmesan.

"PASTA"-TIVELY PERFECT

Most recipes for spaghetti and meatballs have you cook the meatballs and pasta separately and then combine them right before you eat. Not this one! In this recipe, everything cooks all at once, right in the oven. For perfectly tender spaghetti, we fill the baking dish with exactly the right amount of water and marinara sauce, so there's no need to drain the pasta. Covering the baking dish with aluminum foil for the first 30 minutes in the oven traps hot steam and helps the pasta and the meatballs cook evenly. Removing the foil releases the steam. Stirring helps the spaghetti release its starch into the surrounding liquid, thickening the sauce to just the right consistency. And as a bonus, the spaghetti absorbs some of the flavorful sauce as it cooks.

PASTA WITH KALE-BASIL PESTO

You can use lacinato or curly kale in this recipe. You can substitute 1 pound of another short pasta shape for the penne, such as farfalle, rigatoni, ziti, or medium shells, if you like.

PREPARE INGREDIENTS

¼ cup pine nuts

4 quarts water

1 cup fresh basil leaves

2 ounces kale, stemmed and leaves torn into small pieces (about 1 cup) (see photo, right)

½ cup extra-virgin olive oil

¼ cup grated Parmesan cheese (½ ounce), plus extra for serving (see page 13)

1 garlic clove, peeled (see page 94) ▶

½ teaspoon plus 1 tablespoon table salt, measured separately

1 pound penne pasta

GATHER COOKING EQUIPMENT

10-inch skillet

Rubber spatula

Colander

Large pot

Food processor

Wooden spoon

Ladle

Liquid measuring cup

SERVES 4 to 6

TOTAL TIME 45 minutes

LEVEL ◼◻◻

1 Add pine nuts to 10-inch skillet. Toast pine nuts over low heat, using rubber spatula to stir often, until lightly browned and fragrant, 6 to 8 minutes. Turn off heat and slide skillet to cool burner. Let cool for 10 minutes.

2 Set colander in sink. Add water to large pot. Bring to boil over high heat.

3 While water heats, add basil, kale, oil, Parmesan, garlic, ½ teaspoon salt, and pine nuts to food processor. Lock lid into place. Turn on processor and process for 30 seconds. Stop processor, remove lid, and scrape down sides of processor bowl with rubber spatula.

4 Lock lid back into place. Turn on processor and process until mixture is smooth, about 30 seconds. Stop processor, remove lid, and carefully remove processor blade (ask an adult for help).

5 Carefully add pasta and remaining 1 tablespoon salt to boiling water. Cook, stirring often with wooden spoon, until pasta is al dente (tender but still a bit chewy; see page 121), 10 to 12 minutes. Turn off heat.

6 Use ladle to carefully transfer ½ cup pasta cooking water to liquid measuring cup. Ask an adult to drain pasta in colander. Return drained pasta to now-empty pot.

7 Use rubber spatula to scrape pesto into pot with pasta. Add ¼ cup reserved cooking water. Stir until pasta is well coated with pesto. If needed, add remaining ¼ cup reserved cooking water, a little bit at a time, until sauce is loosened slightly and coats pasta well. Serve with extra Parmesan.

HOW TO STEM KALE

Hold end of kale stem in 1 hand. Pinch thumb and index finger of your other hand on either side of stem. Slide your hand down length of stem from bottom to top to strip leaf from stem. Discard stem.

PRESTO, PESTO!

Basil pesto (also called pesto Genovese, after the Italian city Genoa, where it originated) is an Italian sauce traditionally made with fresh basil, pine nuts, garlic, salt, cheese, and olive oil. We keep this version mostly traditional—except for the addition of kale. Its dark leaves turn this pesto a vibrant shade of green, and because raw kale tastes mild, it doesn't change the pesto's flavor. Stirring in some pasta cooking water along with the pesto helps the sauce cling to each and every noodle, so you get maximum pesto flavor in every bite (see page 121 to learn more about the power of pasta cooking water).

ONE-POT GARLICKY SHRIMP PASTA

You can substitute 12 ounces of any short pasta shape for the shells; however, the cup measurements will vary—use 3¾ cups of penne, 3¾ cups of ziti, or 4¾ cups of farfalle. If you love garlic, use the full 8 cloves.

PREPARE INGREDIENTS

- 1 pound frozen peeled and deveined extra-large shrimp (21 to 25 per pound), thawed and tails removed
- ⅛ teaspoon pepper
- ½ teaspoon plus ¾ teaspoon table salt, measured separately
- 1 tablespoon plus 2 tablespoons extra-virgin olive oil, measured separately
- 6–8 garlic cloves, peeled and minced (see page 94) ▶
- ⅛ teaspoon red pepper flakes
- 4½ cups (12 ounces) medium pasta shells
- 3 cups water
- 2 cups chicken broth
- ½ cup bottled clam juice
- 2 tablespoons chopped fresh parsley (see page 67) ▶
- ½ teaspoon grated lemon zest plus 2 tablespoons juice, zested and squeezed from 1 lemon (see page 14) ▶

GATHER COOKING EQUIPMENT

Medium bowl	Tongs
Rubber spatula	Large plate
Dutch oven	

SERVES 4

TOTAL TIME 45 minutes

LEVEL ◼◻◻

"The garlic gave the pasta a really good flavor that enhanced the whole dish."
—Maya, 11

START COOKING!

1 In medium bowl, combine shrimp, pepper, and ½ teaspoon salt. Use rubber spatula to stir until shrimp are evenly coated.

2 In Dutch oven, heat 1 tablespoon oil over medium-high heat until shimmering, about 2 minutes (oil should be hot but not smoking; see page 11). (▶)

3 Add shrimp to pot and use rubber spatula to spread in single layer. Cook shrimp, without stirring, until edges turn pink, about 1 minute.

4 Stir shrimp and cook until pink all over, 30 to 60 seconds. Turn off heat. Use tongs to transfer shrimp to large plate (see photo, below right).

5 Add garlic, pepper flakes, and remaining 2 tablespoons oil to pot. Cook over low heat, stirring often with clean rubber spatula, until garlic is just beginning to turn golden, 4 to 6 minutes.

6 Stir in pasta, water, broth, clam juice, and remaining ¾ teaspoon salt. Increase heat to medium-high and cook, stirring often, for 12 minutes.

7 Continue to cook, stirring constantly and scraping bottom of pot, until pasta is tender and sauce is thickened, 3 to 8 minutes. Turn off heat. (Sauce will continue to thicken as it cools.)

8 Stir in parsley, lemon zest and juice, and shrimp. Let sit until shrimp are heated through, 1 to 2 minutes. Serve.

A "SHRIMP"-LY DELICIOUS PASTA

This one-pot meal features seafood flavor in every bite, thanks to two oceanic ingredients. First: the shrimp. These slightly sweet crustaceans cook through VERY quickly, in just about 2 minutes. We take the cooked shrimp out of the pot before adding the pasta—this way they don't overcook and turn tough and rubbery. The second seafood star: clam juice. This briny liquid, made by cooking clams in salted water, boosts this dish's delicate seafood flavor. Cooking the pasta in a mixture of clam juice and chicken broth (instead of cooking it in a separate pot of water, draining it, and then adding the sauce) lets the dry pasta soak up all that savory, salty flavor.

COOKING SHRIMP

Cook shrimp, without stirring, until edges turn pink, about 1 minute. Stir shrimp and cook until pink all over, 30 to 60 seconds. Turn off heat. Use tongs to transfer shrimp to large plate.

INSTANT MASHED POTATO GNOCCHI
WITH BROWNED BUTTER SAUCE

We developed this recipe using Idahoan Original Mashed Potatoes. Do not use flavored instant mashed potato flakes. It is important to knead the dough for the full 3 minutes in step 3 or else it will be too tender and difficult to roll into ropes. Use a light-colored skillet if you have one—it will be easier to see the butter turn golden brown than if you use a dark-colored skillet.

PREPARE INGREDIENTS

2 cups (4 ounces) plain instant mashed potato flakes

1 cup (5 ounces) all-purpose flour, plus extra for counter

5¼ teaspoons table salt

1 large egg

1½ cups plus 4 quarts water, measured separately

6 tablespoons unsalted butter, cut into six 1-tablespoon pieces

1 tablespoon lemon juice, squeezed from ½ lemon (see page 14)

1 tablespoon chopped fresh parsley (see page 67) ▶

Grated Parmesan cheese (see page 13) ▶

SERVES 4

TOTAL TIME 1¼ hours

LEVEL ▪▫▫

"Rolling out the dough and cutting it into little pieces was fun."
—Nadia, 9

GATHER COOKING EQUIPMENT

2 bowls (1 large, 1 medium)

Whisk

Measuring spoons

Wooden spoon

Rimmed baking sheet

Bench scraper or chef's knife

Ruler

Large pot

12-inch skillet

Rubber spatula

Spider skimmer or slotted spoon

GNOCCHI IN AN INSTANT

Potato gnocchi ("NYOH-kee") are a type of Italian dumpling made with mashed potatoes, flour, and egg. They're fun to make, but they're a real labor of love. For traditional potato gnocchi, you cook, peel, and mash the potatoes—and that's BEFORE you make the dough, shape the gnocchi, and cook them. But with one magic ingredient, gnocchi making is faster and easier. Meet instant mashed potato flakes, which are essentially dehydrated mashed potatoes formed into teeny-tiny flakes. Combining them with flour, salt, egg, and water makes the quickest-ever gnocchi dough. The water hydrates the potato flakes, making the dough soft and easy to roll and giving you tender, pillowy gnocchi.

---

1 In large bowl, whisk together potato flakes, flour, and 2 teaspoons salt. In medium bowl, whisk together egg and 1½ cups water.

2 Add egg mixture to potato flake mixture and stir with wooden spoon until fully combined and mixture forms ball, about 1 minute. Let sit for 3 minutes.

3 Sprinkle extra flour on clean counter and coat your hands with extra flour. Transfer dough to floured counter and use your floured hands to knead until dough has texture of Play-Doh, at least 3 minutes (lightly sprinkle counter with more flour if dough begins to stick). Lightly sprinkle dough with extra flour and let rest on counter for 5 minutes.

4 Sprinkle rimmed baking sheet with extra flour. Use bench scraper to divide dough into 6 equal pieces. Roll and cut gnocchi following photos 1–3, page 130.

5 Add remaining 4 quarts water to large pot. Bring to boil over high heat.

6 While water heats, in 12-inch skillet, melt butter over medium-high heat. When butter is melted, reduce heat to medium-low.

KEEP GOING! →

7 Cook, stirring constantly and scraping bottom of skillet with rubber spatula, until butter solids turn golden brown and butter smells nutty, 6 to 8 minutes. Turn off heat and slide skillet to cool burner. Carefully stir in lemon juice, parsley, and ¼ teaspoon salt (sauce will bubble and foam).

8 When water is boiling, add remaining 1 tablespoon salt to pot. Use spider skimmer to carefully add half of gnocchi to boiling water (see photo 4, below; ask an adult for help).

9 Cook, gently stirring with spider skimmer, until gnocchi float to surface of water, about 1½ minutes. Use spider skimmer to transfer gnocchi to skillet with sauce. Return water to boil and repeat cooking with remaining gnocchi. Turn off heat.

10 Place skillet over medium-high heat. Cook, gently stirring with rubber spatula, until gnocchi are heated through and well coated with sauce, about 2 minutes. Turn off heat. Serve with Parmesan.

HOW TO SHAPE AND COOK GNOCCHI

1 On very lightly floured counter, roll 1 piece of dough into ¾-inch-thick rope, about 18 inches long.

2 Lightly sprinkle rope and bench scraper with extra flour. Use floured bench scraper to cut rope crosswise (the short way) into ¾-inch squares.

3 Transfer gnocchi to lightly floured rimmed baking sheet. Repeat steps 1 through 3 with remaining dough pieces.

4 When ready to cook, add gnocchi to spider skimmer and gently lower into boiling water. Repeat until half of gnocchi are added to pot.

CHEESY BEAN AND TOMATO BAKE

Serve with crusty bread or Garlic Bread (page 162).

PREPARE INGREDIENTS

- 2 (15-ounce) cans white beans, opened
- 1 tablespoon plus 2 tablespoons extra-virgin olive oil, measured separately
- 1 small onion, peeled and chopped fine (see page 93)
- ¾ teaspoon table salt
- 3 garlic cloves, peeled and minced (see page 94) ▶
- 1 teaspoon dried oregano
- Pinch red pepper flakes (optional)
- 1 (28-ounce) can crushed tomatoes, opened
- ⅓ cup water
- Pinch sugar
- ¼ cup grated Parmesan cheese (½ ounce) (see page 13) ▶
- 1 cup shredded mozzarella cheese (4 ounces) (see page 13) ▶
- ½ cup panko bread crumbs

GATHER COOKING EQUIPMENT

- Colander
- 12-inch ovensafe skillet
- Wooden spoon
- Small bowl
- Spoon
- Oven mitts
- Cooling rack

SERVES 4 to 6

TOTAL TIME 1 hour

LEVEL ■■□

> *"Delicious! Just like Grandma's chicken Parm, but minus the chicken plus the beans. I love this!"*
> —Adia, 11

1 Adjust oven rack to middle position and heat oven to 475 degrees. Set colander in sink. Pour beans into colander. Rinse beans with cold water and shake colander to drain well.

2 In 12-inch ovensafe skillet, heat 1 tablespoon oil over medium heat until shimmering, about 2 minutes (oil should be hot but not smoking; see page 11). ▶

3 Add onion and salt and cook, stirring often with wooden spoon, until onion is softened, about 5 minutes. Add garlic, oregano, and pepper flakes (if using) and cook, stirring constantly, for 30 seconds.

4 Stir in tomatoes, water, and sugar. Bring to boil. Reduce heat to medium-low and simmer (small bubbles should break often across surface of mixture), stirring occasionally, until slightly thickened, about 10 minutes.

5 Add drained beans to skillet and stir to coat with sauce. Cook, stirring occasionally, until beans are warmed through, about 5 minutes. Turn off heat and slide skillet to cool burner.

6 Stir Parmesan and half of mozzarella into beans. Spread beans into even layer. Sprinkle remaining mozzarella evenly over top.

7 In small bowl, combine panko and remaining 2 tablespoons oil. Use spoon to stir until panko is coated with oil. Sprinkle panko evenly over top of cheese.

8 Ask an adult to transfer skillet to oven. Bake until cheese is melted and panko is well browned, 5 to 8 minutes.

9 Ask an adult to use oven mitts to remove skillet from oven and place on cooling rack (skillet will be VERY hot). Place oven mitt on skillet handle so you remember handle is HOT. Let beans cool for 5 minutes. Serve.

SHAKE UP YOUR BEAN ROUTINE

This cheesy, saucy dish includes the best parts of baked ziti, but with creamy, protein-packed white beans swapped in for the traditional pasta. A simple tomato sauce keeps things moist—we highly recommend sopping up any extra sauce with some crusty bread or Garlic Bread (page 162). Gooey mozzarella and umami-packed Parmesan add plenty of cheesy flavor in every bite while a panko bread crumb topping gives this bake a final layer of crunch.

STIR-FRIED RICE CAKES WITH BOK CHOY AND SNOW PEAS

If using frozen Korean rice cakes, be sure to defrost them before cooking. You can find rice cakes and gochujang, a spicy Korean chile paste, in the Korean section of many supermarkets or in Korean markets. If you like things spicy, use the full amount of gochujang.

PREPARE INGREDIENTS

- 3 tablespoons soy sauce
- 1 tablespoon sugar
- 1 tablespoon toasted sesame oil
- 1 tablespoon hoisin sauce
- ½–1 teaspoon gochujang paste
- 4 heads baby bok choy (4 ounces each)
- 1 tablespoon vegetable oil
- 3 scallions, root ends trimmed and scallions cut into 1-inch pieces
- 3 garlic cloves, peeled and minced (see page 94) ▶
- 1 pound Korean rice cakes (sliced or tube-shaped)
- ⅓ cup water
- 4 ounces snow peas, strings removed and cut in half crosswise (the short way)

GATHER COOKING EQUIPMENT

Small bowl

Whisk

Cutting board

Chef's knife

Ruler

12-inch nonstick skillet with lid

Wooden spoon

Oven mitts

SERVES 4

TOTAL TIME 35 minutes

LEVEL ◼◻

" If you like spicy, this is a good recipe."
—Emmett, 9

1 In small bowl, whisk soy sauce, sugar, sesame oil, hoisin, and gochujang until combined. Set aside.

2 Cut, wash, and chop bok choy following photo, right.

3 Heat vegetable oil in 12-inch nonstick skillet over medium-high heat until shimmering, about 2 minutes (oil should be hot but not smoking; see page 11). (▶)

4 Add scallions to skillet and cook, stirring occasionally with wooden spoon, until scallions are just beginning to brown, about 2 minutes.

5 Add garlic to skillet and cook for 30 seconds. Stir in rice cakes, separating any that are stuck together, and bok choy. Add water and cover with lid. Cook, covered, until bok choy is bright green and liquid has begun to evaporate, about 3 minutes.

6 Use oven mitts to remove lid. Add soy sauce mixture and snow peas to skillet and stir until well combined. Cook, stirring occasionally, until sauce is thickened, 1 to 2 minutes. Turn off heat. Serve.

HOW TO PREP BABY BOK CHOY

Place 1 baby bok choy on cutting board. Use chef's knife to cut bok choy in half lengthwise (the long way). Repeat with remaining bok choy. Rinse and dry bok choy. Place bok choy on cutting board, cut side down. Trim root end from bottom of each bok choy. Discard root end. Cut each bok choy crosswise (the short way) into 1-inch pieces.

ALL ABOUT KOREAN RICE CAKES

The star ingredient in this stir-fry is Korean rice cakes, called tteok ("DOK") in Korean. There are many different varieties of tteok in Korean cuisine. This recipe uses chewy garaetteok ("yeah-reh-DOK"), a type of rice cake made from a mixture of rice flour and water that's pounded and kneaded into a pliable dough and then rolled into a long, thick cylinder. Then, it's sliced into thin, oblong disks or cut into smaller cylinders. The mild-tasting garaetteok provide a blank canvas for the flavorful sauce and add a satisfyingly chewy texture to this simple stir-fry.

THAI RED CURRY WITH BELL PEPPERS AND TOFU

Serve this dish with white rice.

PREPARE INGREDIENTS

14 ounces extra-firm tofu, cut into ¾-inch cubes (see photos, right)

1 (8-ounce) can sliced bamboo shoots, opened

1 (14-ounce) can coconut milk, opened

1½ tablespoons fish sauce

1 tablespoon packed light brown sugar

1 tablespoon Thai red curry paste

1 teaspoon grated lime zest plus 1 tablespoon juice, zested and squeezed from 1 lime (see page 14), plus lime wedges for serving

2 garlic cloves, peeled and minced (see page 94) ▶

1 teaspoon grated fresh ginger (see page 14) ▶

1 teaspoon plus 1 tablespoon vegetable oil, measured separately

2 red bell peppers, stemmed, seeded, and sliced thin (see page 95) ▶

¼ cup torn fresh basil

GATHER COOKING EQUIPMENT

Rimmed baking sheet	Whisk
Paper towels	12-inch nonstick skillet
Colander	Rubber spatula
2 bowls (1 medium, 1 small)	

SERVES 4 to 6

TOTAL TIME 50 minutes

LEVEL ■■□

"I had never eaten bamboo before, and it was yummy."
—Catie, 10

1   Line rimmed baking sheet with 3 layers of paper towels. Spread tofu cubes on paper towels and let drain for 20 minutes.

2   While tofu drains, set colander in sink. Pour bamboo shoots into colander. Rinse with cold water and shake colander to drain well. Set aside.

3   In medium bowl, whisk together coconut milk, fish sauce, brown sugar, red curry paste, and lime zest and juice. In small bowl, combine garlic, ginger, and 1 teaspoon oil.

4   When tofu is ready, gently pat dry with more paper towels.

5   In 12-inch nonstick skillet, heat remaining 1 tablespoon oil over medium-high heat until shimmering, about 2 minutes (oil should be hot but not smoking; see page 11). (▶)

6   Add bell peppers and cook, stirring often with rubber spatula, until crisp-tender, about 2 minutes.

7   Push bell peppers to edge of skillet, clearing space in center. Add garlic mixture to center of skillet and cook, stirring and mashing with rubber spatula, for 30 seconds. Stir garlic mixture into bell peppers.

8   Add tofu and bamboo shoots to skillet. Whisk coconut milk mixture to recombine, then pour into skillet. Cook, stirring often, until sauce is thickened, 3 to 4 minutes. Turn off heat. Sprinkle with basil. Serve with lime wedges.

HOW TO CUBE TOFU

1 Place tofu on cutting board. Use chef's knife to slice block of tofu lengthwise (the long way) into four ¾-inch-thick slabs.

2 Lay slabs flat and cut each slab in half lengthwise to make 2 long sticks (about ¾ inch thick). Cut tofu sticks crosswise (the short way) into ¾-inch cubes.

A FLURRY OF CURRY

"Curry" can refer to curry powder (a blend of ground spices); curry leaves (used in some Indian dishes); or a saucy, spiced stew that can be found in cuisines all over the world, including in Thailand. Thai curry, called gaeng ("gang"), is often flavored with a potent paste of aromatics (such as garlic and lemongrass), herbs, spices, chile peppers, and other savory ingredients. Some of the most widely used Thai curry pastes are red, green, massaman, panang, and yellow.

5 SIDES

SPICE-ROASTED CARROTS

Colorful rainbow carrots are especially fun to use in this recipe, but any medium-size carrots will work. Carrots sold in a bunch with their green tops attached are the most likely to be similar in size, which helps them cook evenly. If you can't find them, you can use medium-size bagged carrots that are similar in size to one another. You can sprinkle chopped fresh cilantro, mint, or parsley on top of your carrots instead of chopped carrot tops, if you prefer.

PREPARE INGREDIENTS

- 1½ pounds medium carrots with tops
- 2 tablespoons extra-virgin olive oil
- ½ teaspoon table salt
- ½ teaspoon paprika
- ¼ teaspoon pepper
- ¼ teaspoon ground cinnamon
- ¼ teaspoon garlic powder
- Pinch cayenne pepper (optional)

GATHER COOKING EQUIPMENT

Rimmed baking sheet

Aluminum foil

Cutting board

Chef's knife

1-tablespoon measuring spoon

Vegetable peeler

Small bowl

Spoon

Oven mitts

Cooling rack

Tongs

Serving platter

SERVES 4

TOTAL TIME 50 minutes

LEVEL

"The mix of spices was perfect. The smell of the carrots filled the room like cookies do—in a good way."
—Addy, 10

START COOKING!

1   Adjust oven rack to middle position and heat oven to 425 degrees. Line rimmed baking sheet with aluminum foil.

2   Place carrots on cutting board and use chef's knife to trim green tops from carrots, leaving about 1 inch of greens attached. Chop 1 tablespoon carrot tops and set aside for garnish. Discard remaining tops or save for another use. Use vegetable peeler to peel carrots. Transfer carrots to foil-lined baking sheet.

3   In small bowl, use spoon to stir oil, salt, paprika, pepper, cinnamon, garlic powder, and cayenne (if using) until combined.

4   Drizzle oil mixture over carrots. Use your hands to toss and rub carrots until evenly coated. Spread carrots into even layer on baking sheet. Wash your hands.

5   Cover baking sheet tightly with aluminum foil. Place baking sheet in oven and roast for 15 minutes.

6   Use oven mitts to remove baking sheet from oven and place on cooling rack (ask an adult for help). Ask an adult to remove foil (be careful as steam is released). Use tongs to flip carrots.

7   Use oven mitts to return baking sheet to oven and continue to roast, uncovered, until thick ends of carrots are tender, 10 to 15 minutes.

8   Use oven mitts to remove baking sheet from oven and place on cooling rack (ask an adult for help). Let carrots cool for 5 minutes.

9   Use tongs to transfer carrots to serving platter. Sprinkle with reserved chopped carrot tops. Serve.

THE DREAM STEAM

If you roast whole carrots uncovered, their outsides will dry out and turn leathery before their insides are cooked through and tender. Plus, any spices will burn and taste bitter! The solution? Cook your carrots in two steps.

Step 1: Steam

Carrots contain a lot of water. As they cook, some of that water turns into steam. Covering the baking sheet tightly with foil traps the steam, and the moist heat helps the carrots cook evenly—and won't dry them out.

Step 2: Brown

Removing the foil partway through cooking lets the steam escape and dries the outside of the carrots. Once the outsides are dry, they begin to turn brown, creating lots of new (and delicious!) flavor molecules.

HONEY BUTTER CORN

PREPARE INGREDIENTS

1 pound frozen corn

2 tablespoons vegetable oil

½ teaspoon table salt

¼ teaspoon pepper

3 tablespoons unsalted butter, cut into 3 pieces

2 tablespoons honey

1 teaspoon minced fresh thyme (see page 67) ▶

GATHER COOKING EQUIPMENT

Rimmed baking sheet

Paper towels

12-inch nonstick skillet

Wooden spoon

SERVES 4

TOTAL TIME 45 minutes

LEVEL ■■□□

1 Line rimmed baking sheet with triple layer of paper towels. Spread corn on paper towel–lined baking sheet and let thaw for 20 minutes. Gently pat corn dry with more paper towels.

2 In 12-inch nonstick skillet, heat oil over medium-high heat until shimmering, about 2 minutes (oil should be hot but not smoking; see page 11). ▶

3 Add corn, salt, and pepper and cook, stirring occasionally with wooden spoon, until corn is spotty brown, 8 to 10 minutes.

4 Turn off heat and slide skillet to cool burner. Stir in butter, honey, and thyme until butter is melted, about 30 seconds. Serve.

"The honey makes a sweet addition to the already delicious corn."
—Michael, 13

EASY FREEZE-Y

While it's tough to beat fresh-picked sweet corn in the summer, frozen corn comes pretty close—and it means that you can enjoy this dish all year long! To keep frozen corn as sweet as possible, it's picked when it's perfectly ripe and sweet. The husks and silk are removed, and then the kernels are cut from the cobs, cooked very quickly, and, finally, frozen at a supercold temperature. In this recipe, it's important to pat the thawed kernels dry before you start cooking. Not only will this prevent messy splattering in the skillet, but dry kernels will also brown more easily—and browning adds even more flavor to this sweet side dish.

SESAME GREEN BEANS

PREPARE INGREDIENTS

- 1 tablespoon soy sauce
- 2 teaspoons honey
- 2 teaspoons unseasoned rice vinegar
- 2 teaspoons toasted sesame oil
- 2 teaspoons sesame seeds
- 1 tablespoon vegetable oil
- 1 pound green beans, trimmed (see photo, right)

GATHER COOKING EQUIPMENT

- 2 small bowls
- Whisk
- 12-inch skillet with lid
- Rubber spatula
- Oven mitts
- Serving dish

"The sesame seeds added a great texture."
—Caia, 10

SERVES 4

TOTAL TIME 30 minutes

LEVEL ◾◾◻

1 In small bowl, whisk soy sauce, honey, vinegar, and sesame oil until combined. Set aside.

2 In 12-inch skillet, toast sesame seeds over medium-low heat, stirring often with rubber spatula, until seeds turn golden brown, 3 to 5 minutes. Turn off heat. Transfer seeds to second small bowl. Set aside.

3 Heat vegetable oil in now-empty skillet over medium heat until shimmering, about 1 minute (oil should be hot but not smoking; see page 11). ▶

4 Add green beans and cook, stirring occasionally, until just beginning to brown, about 2 minutes.

5 Cover skillet with lid and reduce heat to medium-low. Cook green beans for 4 minutes. Use oven mitts to remove lid. Stir green beans. Replace lid and continue to cook until spotty brown and crisp-tender, about 3 minutes.

6 Use oven mitts to remove lid. Carefully stir in soy sauce mixture (sauce will bubble and foam) and cook until liquid is mostly evaporated, about 1 minute. Turn off heat.

7 Transfer green beans to serving dish. Sprinkle with toasted sesame seeds. Serve.

HOW TO TRIM GREEN BEANS

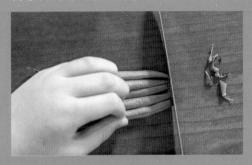

To make trimming green beans easy, line up several green beans on cutting board and cut off tough ends. Repeat on other end of beans.

GETTING TOASTY

Toasting sesame seeds—gently cooking them until they're golden brown and fragrant—creates a nutty, slightly crunchy topping for these green beans. As the sesame seeds heat up, their proteins and sugars react to create new compounds with a brown color and a nutty, toasty smell. (You can use this same toasting technique with just about any seeds or nuts.) And you might have spotted another "toasted sesame" ingredient in this recipe: toasted sesame oil. It's made by pressing—you guessed it!—toasted sesame seeds to release the golden-brown oil inside of them. Give your toasted sesame oil a sniff. Does it smell like the toasted sesame seeds?

WATERMELON AND CHERRY TOMATO SALAD

We like the color of yellow cherry tomatoes in this recipe, but you can substitute red cherry tomatoes, if desired. You can use precut watermelon sold in containers at the grocery store, or ask an adult to help you peel and prep the fruit before cutting it into 1-inch pieces.

PREPARE INGREDIENTS

- 2 tablespoons extra-virgin olive oil
- 1 small shallot, peeled and minced (see page 93) ▶
- ½ teaspoon grated lemon zest plus 1½ tablespoons juice, zested and squeezed from ½ lemon (see page 14) ▶
- ¼ teaspoon table salt
- ¼ teaspoon pepper
- 4 cups 1-inch seedless watermelon pieces
- 2 cups (12 ounces) yellow cherry tomatoes, halved
- ¼ cup fresh basil leaves, torn into small pieces
- 6 ounces fresh mozzarella cheese, torn into 1-inch pieces

GATHER COOKING EQUIPMENT

Large serving bowl

Whisk

Rubber spatula

SERVES 4

TOTAL TIME 20 minutes

LEVEL ◼◻◻

"We weren't sure that watermelon would taste good with tomatoes and cheese, but it does."
—Michael, 11 & Isabella, 9

START COOKING!

1 In large serving bowl, whisk together oil, shallot, lemon zest and juice, salt, and pepper.

2 Add watermelon, tomatoes, and basil to bowl. Use rubber spatula to toss until coated with dressing.

3 Sprinkle mozzarella evenly over top. Serve.

THE SWEETER SIDE OF SALAD

Watermelon and tomatoes . . . together in a salad?! Yes, these garden neighbors can also be friends on your plate. This colorful side dish mixes sweet watermelon and savory tomatoes with herby basil, creamy fresh mozzarella, and a tangy lemon dressing. All those flavors combine into a perfectly balanced—and very refreshing—side dish. Once you try it, you'll see your favorite summer fruits (surprise—tomatoes are actually fruits!) in a whole new light.

GARLIC-FETA CUCUMBER SALAD

PREPARE INGREDIENTS

3 tablespoons extra-virgin olive oil

4 teaspoons red wine vinegar

1 small garlic clove, peeled and minced (see page 94) ▶

¼ teaspoon dried oregano

¼ teaspoon table salt

⅛ teaspoon pepper

1 English cucumber, sliced into thin half-moons (see page 92) ▶

½ cup crumbled feta cheese (2 ounces)

2 tablespoons chopped fresh mint (see page 67) ▶

GATHER COOKING EQUIPMENT

Large serving bowl

Whisk

Rubber spatula

SERVES 4

TOTAL TIME 45 minutes

LEVEL ◼◻◻

START COOKING!

1 In large serving bowl, whisk together oil, vinegar, garlic, oregano, salt, and pepper.

2 Add cucumber to bowl and use rubber spatula to toss until coated with dressing. Let sit for 30 minutes.

3 Add feta and mint to bowl and gently stir to combine. Season with salt and pepper to taste (see page 58). Serve.

WORTH THE WAIT

This simple salad comes together quickly—in just about the time it takes to measure and chop everything. But the most important ingredient might be patience. Letting the cucumber soak for half an hour gives it time to absorb some of the dressing, making every bite even more flavorful. (If you served your salad right away, the dressing would just sit on the surface—this technique seasons the cucumber inside and out.) But don't let your cucumber sit for too long! It's full of water and will release its liquid as it sits—leave it for more than 30 minutes and you'll be left with a very watery salad.

"I loved the fresh mint smell and taste."
—Avery, 10

BRAISED RED POTATOES

Use small red potatoes measuring about 1½ inches in diameter for this recipe.

PREPARE INGREDIENTS

1½ pounds small red potatoes, unpeeled, halved

2 cups water

3 tablespoons unsalted butter, cut into 3 pieces

3 garlic cloves, peeled (see page 94)

¾ teaspoon table salt

1 teaspoon lemon juice, squeezed from ½ lemon (see page 14) ▶

¼ teaspoon pepper

2 tablespoons minced fresh chives

GATHER COOKING EQUIPMENT

12-inch nonstick skillet with lid

Oven mitts

Slotted spoon

Cutting board

Fork

Small bowl

Rubber spatula

SERVES 4 to 6

TOTAL TIME 55 minutes

LEVEL ▪▪◻◻

"This recipe is delicious. The seasoning is incredible, and the texture of the potatoes is perfect."
—Benjamin, 11

1 In 12-inch nonstick skillet, arrange potatoes in single layer, cut side down. Add water, butter, garlic, and salt to skillet. Bring to simmer over medium-high heat (small bubbles should break often across surface of mixture).

2 Reduce heat to medium; cover skillet with lid; and cook until potatoes are just tender, about 15 minutes.

3 Use oven mitts to remove lid. Use slotted spoon to transfer garlic to cutting board.

4 Increase heat to medium-high and cook potatoes, uncovered, until water evaporates and cut sides of potatoes turn spotty brown, 12 to 18 minutes (see photo, above right).

5 While potatoes cook, let garlic cool slightly, about 5 minutes. Use fork to mash garlic to paste. Transfer garlic paste to small bowl. Stir in lemon juice and pepper until well combined.

6 When potatoes are ready, turn off heat. Add garlic mixture and chives to skillet and use rubber spatula to stir until potatoes are well coated. Serve.

HOW TO CHECK POTATOES

The easiest way to check if potatoes are browned is to use a fork: Pick up a potato and look for browning on the bottom.

"BRAISING" THE TRAIL

To create these crispy-on-the-outside, creamy-on-the-inside potatoes, we use two different cooking techniques. First, we braise the potatoes. "Braising" means simmering in a small amount of liquid in a covered pot or skillet—this step cooks the potatoes' interiors until they're tender. Then, it's time to brown. Uncovering the skillet and cranking up the heat allows trapped steam to escape and the water to evaporate. On the hot, dry surface of the skillet, the cut sides of the potatoes turn beautifully brown and crispy. While the spuds finish cooking, we mash the softened garlic into a paste so that it can coat each and every potato.

THE BASICS:

COOKING RICE

There are thousands of different types of rice grown around the world. Rice can be a great standalone side dish or a companion to curries (see page 136) and stir-fries.

COMPARING RICE

White Rice versus Brown Rice	Every grain of rice starts out surrounded by a protective covering (called the husk). If you remove the husk, you've got a grain of brown rice. To make white rice, manufacturers remove a few more layers from brown rice—namely the bran and the germ. The bran and germ give brown rice its color and a boost of nutritious fiber but also cause it to absorb water more slowly.
Long-Grain versus Short-Grain	In the grocery store, you'll see packages of long-grain rice and short-grain rice. The names pretty much explain it: Long-grain rice is longer and skinnier. Short-grain rice is shorter and thicker. But there's a bit more to the story—long-grain rice tends to cook up as fluffy, separate grains, while short-grain varieties, such as the sushi rice in Cucumber-Avocado Maki (page 88), turn slightly sticky when they're cooked.

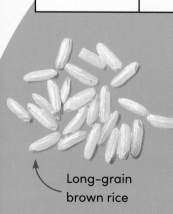

Short-grain white rice

Long-grain white rice

Long-grain brown rice

Short-grain brown rice

RINSE YOUR WHITE RICE

Many recipes tell you to rinse white rice before cooking. Rinsing removes starch from the surface of the rice and helps it cook up as fluffy, individual grains rather than a sticky blob. You don't need to rinse brown rice—its outer bran layer keeps its starch on the inside.

To Rinse White Rice:

Set fine-mesh strainer over large bowl and set in sink. Place rice in strainer. Rinse rice under cold running water, emptying bowl a few times as it fills, until water in bowl is clear, 1½ to 2 minutes. Shake strainer to drain rice well. Discard water in bowl.

TWO WAYS TO COOK RICE

Absorption Method

In this method, the rice absorbs (soaks up) all the liquid as it cooks—you add exactly the amount of liquid needed to turn the rice tender. Bonus: no draining needed! See it in action in Lowcountry Red Rice (page 154).

Pasta Method

In this method, you cook rice just like you would cook pasta: in a big pot of boiling water. When the rice is tender, you drain it in a colander in the sink. This method helps the rice cook evenly, and it's also faster than the absorption method. Try it for yourself in Brown Rice with Lime Dressing (page 156).

LOWCOUNTRY RED RICE

If you like things spicy, add the full amount of cayenne pepper.

PREPARE INGREDIENTS

1 (14.5-ounce) can diced tomatoes, opened

3 slices bacon, cut in half crosswise (the short way)

1 onion, peeled and chopped fine (see page 93)

1 green bell pepper, stemmed, seeded, and chopped fine (see page 95)

1 celery rib, chopped fine

¾ teaspoon table salt

1½ cups long-grain white rice, rinsed (see page 153)

4 garlic cloves, peeled and minced (see page 94)

1 tablespoon tomato paste

⅛–¼ teaspoon cayenne pepper

2 cups chicken broth

GATHER COOKING EQUIPMENT

Colander	Wooden spoon
Plate	Oven mitts
Paper towels	Dish towel
Large saucepan with lid	Fork
Tongs	Serving dish

SERVES 6

TOTAL TIME 1¼ hours

LEVEL ▪■□

"The rice had so much flavor. The touch of cayenne added just enough spice."
—Jacob, 8

START COOKING!

1 Set colander in sink. Pour diced tomatoes into colander. Shake colander to drain well.

2 Line plate with paper towels and place on counter next to stovetop. Cook bacon in large saucepan over medium heat, flipping occasionally with tongs, until crispy, 7 to 9 minutes. Turn off heat. Use tongs to transfer bacon to paper towel–lined plate. Set aside to cool.

3 Add onion, bell pepper, celery, and salt to bacon fat left in saucepan. Cook over medium heat, stirring occasionally with wooden spoon, until vegetables are softened, about 5 minutes.

4 Add rice and cook, stirring often, until grains start to look slightly clear on ends, about 2 minutes. Stir in garlic, tomato paste, and cayenne and cook for 30 seconds.

5 Stir in drained tomatoes and broth and bring to boil. Reduce heat to low; cover with lid; and cook until liquid is absorbed and rice is tender, about 20 minutes.

6 Turn off heat and slide saucepan to cool burner. Use oven mitts to place folded dish towel underneath lid. Let rice sit, covered, for 10 minutes.

7 Crumble cooled bacon into small pieces. Remove lid and fluff rice with fork. Season with salt to taste (see page 58). Transfer rice to serving dish and sprinkle with bacon. Serve.

THAT'S SOME NICE RICE

A popular side dish in the Lowcountry coastal regions of South Carolina and Georgia, red rice is hearty, savory, and a little bit smoky. It's also known as Charleston red rice, named for Charleston, South Carolina, and Gullah red rice, named for the Gullah Geechee people that descend from West and Central Africans who were enslaved and brought to the Lowcountry to work on rice plantations in the 1700s. There are many versions of red rice, but most include onion, green bell pepper, and celery (known as the "holy trinity" of vegetables in many types of Southern cooking); a smoky pork product, such as bacon or sausage; and tomatoes, which give this dish its namesake color.

Onion, green bell peppers, and celery are often called the "holy trinity" of vegetables in Southern cooking.

BROWN RICE WITH LIME DRESSING

PREPARE INGREDIENTS

4	quarts water
1½	cups long-grain brown rice
1	tablespoon table salt
2	tablespoons lime juice, squeezed from 1 lime (see page 14)
1	tablespoon honey
½	teaspoon ground cumin
¼	cup extra-virgin olive oil
¼	cup chopped fresh cilantro (see page 67)

GATHER COOKING EQUIPMENT

Colander

Large pot

Wooden spoon

Large serving bowl

Whisk

SERVES **4 to 6**

TOTAL TIME **55 minutes**

LEVEL

"YUM YUM YUM
YUM YUM!!!
I loved every bite!!!"
—Lucy, 11

1   Set colander in sink. Add water to large pot. Bring to boil over high heat.

2   Carefully add rice and salt to boiling water. Cook, stirring occasionally with wooden spoon, until rice is tender, 25 to 35 minutes.

3   While rice cooks, in large serving bowl, whisk together lime juice, honey, and cumin. While whisking constantly, slowly pour in oil until combined.

4   When rice is ready, turn off heat. Ask an adult to drain rice in colander.

5   Transfer rice to bowl with dressing. Add cilantro and gently stir until well combined. Season with salt to taste (see page 58). Serve.

HOW RICE COOKS

As grains of rice simmer in hot water, they turn from hard to tender. During cooking, tiny starch granules in the center of the rice absorb water, making the rice soften and puff up (if you look closely, you'll see that grains of cooked rice are a little larger than grains of uncooked rice). Brown rice takes longer to cook than white rice—its outer layer (called the bran) absorbs water more slowly, so grains of brown rice need more time to soften. Grains of white rice, which are made of just a starchy endosperm layer, absorb water much more quickly. In this recipe, we cook brown rice using the pasta method—simmering it in a large pot of water until it's tender and then draining it in a colander (learn more on page 153). Tossing the just-cooked rice with our lime dressing allows the warm grains of rice to absorb some of the dressing, giving the rice an extra layer of flavor.

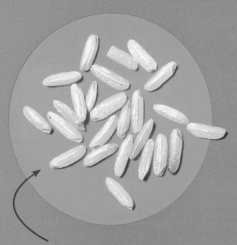

Grains of brown rice

PEARL COUSCOUS WITH HERBS

Pearl couscous, also called Israeli couscous, has round grains that are much larger than grains of North African couscous.

PREPARE INGREDIENTS

1½ cups pearl couscous

1 tablespoon plus 1 tablespoon extra-virgin olive oil, measured separately

1¾ cups water

½ teaspoon table salt

1 tablespoon finely chopped fresh parsley, mint, basil, or cilantro (see page 67) ▶

GATHER COOKING EQUIPMENT

Large saucepan with lid

Wooden spoon

Oven mitts

SERVES 4 to 6

TOTAL TIME 30 minutes

LEVEL ◾◽◽

"It was a little scary with the hot pan and boiling water, but I knew I could do it."
—Nadia, 9

START COOKING!

1 In large saucepan, combine couscous and 1 tablespoon oil. Cook over medium heat, stirring often with wooden spoon, until about half of grains are golden brown, 5 to 7 minutes.

2 Carefully stir in water and salt. Increase heat to high and bring to boil. Reduce heat to medium-low, cover saucepan with lid, and cook for 5 minutes.

3 Use oven mitts to remove lid. Stir couscous. Replace lid and continue to cook, stirring 1 or 2 more times, until water is absorbed and couscous is tender, 3 to 5 minutes. Turn off heat and slide saucepan to cool burner.

4 Let couscous sit, covered, for 3 minutes. Use oven mitts to remove lid. Stir in parsley and remaining 1 tablespoon oil until well combined. Season with salt to taste (see page 58). Serve.

DUCK, DUCK, COUSCOUS!

Pearl couscous (called "p'titim" ["ptih-TIM"] in Hebrew) was originally invented in Israel. Just looking at it, you might think pearl couscous is a grain, similar to rice or barley. But it's actually a pasta! Like making many types of Italian pasta, making couscous starts by mixing flour and water to form a dough. Then, the dough gets shaped into tiny spheres. While most pasta is dried before it's packaged, pearl couscous is also toasted, giving it a slightly nuttier flavor than pasta or even North African couscous. In this recipe, we double down on nuttiness by toasting the dry couscous in a bit of oil before cooking it the rest of the way using the absorption method (see page 153).

MAKE IT YOUR WAY!

There are lots of ways to dress up this simple side dish: Try swapping out the herbs for sliced scallions or adding a squeeze of lemon or lime juice. You can also stir in thawed frozen peas; crumbled feta cheese; sliced olives; chopped sun-dried tomatoes or jarred roasted red peppers; and/or chopped tender greens, such as baby spinach or baby kale.

CURRIED CHICKPEAS WITH YOGURT

PREPARE INGREDIENTS

2 (15-ounce) cans chickpeas, opened

2 tablespoons plus 1 tablespoon extra-virgin olive oil, measured separately

1 onion, peeled and chopped fine (see page 93) ▶

¼ teaspoon table salt

2 garlic cloves, peeled and minced (see page 94) ▶

½ teaspoon curry powder

1 cup chicken or vegetable broth

¼ cup plain whole-milk yogurt

2 tablespoons finely chopped fresh cilantro (see page 67) ▶

2 teaspoons lime juice, squeezed from ½ lime (see page 14) ▶

GATHER COOKING EQUIPMENT

Colander

12-inch skillet with lid

Wooden spoon

Oven mitts

SERVES 6

TOTAL TIME 40 minutes

LEVEL ■■□

"This recipe was amazing. If I could, I would eat it for breakfast, lunch, and dinner."
—Kinison, 10

1 Set colander in sink. Pour chickpeas into colander and rinse with cold water. Shake colander to drain well.

2 In 12-inch skillet, heat 2 tablespoons oil over medium heat until shimmering, about 2 minutes (oil should be hot but not smoking; see page 11). ▶

3 Add onion and salt and cook, stirring occasionally with wooden spoon, until onion is softened and lightly browned, 5 to 7 minutes. Stir in garlic and curry powder and cook for 1 minute.

4 Stir in drained chickpeas and broth and bring to simmer (small bubbles should break often across surface of mixture). Cover with lid and cook until chickpeas are warmed through and flavors have combined, about 7 minutes.

5 Use oven mitts to remove lid. Increase heat to medium-high and cook until nearly all liquid has evaporated, 2 to 4 minutes. Turn off heat and slide skillet to cool burner.

6 Stir in yogurt, cilantro, and lime juice. Drizzle with remaining 1 tablespoon oil. Serve.

TRY IT THIS WAY!

CHICKPEAS WITH GARLIC AND BASIL

Leave out curry powder and yogurt. Use **2 tablespoons finely chopped fresh basil** instead of cilantro and **2 teaspoons lemon juice** instead of lime juice.

GET CURIOUS ABOUT CURRY POWDER

Curry powder is a mixture of sweet and savory spices, typically some combination of turmeric (for that signature yellow color), coriander, cumin, black pepper, cardamom, ginger, garlic, cinnamon, chile powder, and fenugreek (a nutty-tasting seed). While we might associate curry powder with Indian food—and you'll see many of its spices in Indian cuisines—it's actually a British invention and isn't used in traditional Indian dishes. Cooking the curry powder in hot oil for just 1 minute unlocks even more of the spices' flavors and infuses the olive oil with them. This cooking technique is known as "blooming" spices (see page 59).

GARLIC BREAD

A 12-by-5-inch loaf of supermarket Italian bread, which has a soft, thin crust, works best here. Do not use a rustic or crusty artisan-style loaf—it will be too hard and tough.

PREPARE INGREDIENTS

- 1 (12-by-5-inch) loaf soft Italian bread (about 1 pound)
- 1 teaspoon garlic powder
- 1 teaspoon water
- 8 tablespoons unsalted butter, cut into 8 pieces and softened (see page 12) ▶
- 4 garlic cloves, peeled and minced (see page 94) ▶
- ½ teaspoon table salt
- ⅛ teaspoon pepper
- ⅛ teaspoon sugar

GATHER COOKING EQUIPMENT

Cutting board

Bread knife

Medium bowl

Fork

Butter knife

Rimmed baking sheet

Oven mitts

Cooling rack

Tongs

SERVES 8

TOTAL TIME 45 minutes

LEVEL ▪️◻️◻️

"This garlic bread is very delicious, and it's very good with spaghetti!"
—Jaycee, 11

1   Adjust oven rack to middle position and heat oven to 450 degrees. Place bread on cutting board and use bread knife to cut bread in half (see photo, right; ask an adult for help).

2   In medium bowl, use fork to stir together garlic powder and water. Add softened butter, minced garlic, salt, pepper, and sugar. Stir and mash butter mixture until well combined.

3   Use butter knife to spread cut sides of bread evenly with butter mixture. Transfer bread, buttered sides up, to rimmed baking sheet.

4   Place baking sheet in oven. Bake until bread is golden brown and toasted, 8 to 10 minutes.

5   Use oven mitts to remove baking sheet from oven and place on cooling rack (ask an adult for help). Let garlic bread cool on baking sheet for 5 minutes.

6   Use tongs to transfer garlic bread to cutting board. Cut each half into 8 slices (ask an adult for help). Serve warm.

HOW TO CUT THE LOAF

Ask an adult to do this step for you if you're not comfortable with a bread knife.

Hold top of bread steady with 1 hand at 1 end of loaf. Using sawing motion, use bread knife to cut loaf in half horizontally. Keep your top hand flat and move it along top of loaf as you slice.

GARLIC GALORE

Combining the powers of two ingredients—fresh garlic and garlic powder—gives this garlic bread the most garlicky flavor possible. Mincing fresh garlic into tiny pieces creates a whole lot of a compound called allicin ("AL-ih-sin"), which is what gives garlic its signature sharp smell and taste. Garlic powder is made by drying out and grinding up whole garlic cloves—a process that gives garlic powder a slightly different flavor that's similar to roasted garlic. Bonus: If you mix garlic powder with water, it also creates allicin, adding yet another boost of garlicky goodness!

CHEDDAR-CHIVE BISCUITS

We like the look of yellow cheddar in these biscuits (fun fact: Yellow cheddar is actually orange!), but white cheddar works just fine.

PREPARE INGREDIENTS

- 2 cups (10 ounces) all-purpose flour, plus extra for counter
- 2 teaspoons sugar
- 2 teaspoons baking powder
- 1 teaspoon Old Bay seasoning
- ½ teaspoon table salt
- ¼ cup shredded extra-sharp cheddar cheese (1 ounce) (see page 13) ▶
- ¼ cup grated Parmesan cheese (½ ounce) (see page 13) ▶
- 2 tablespoons minced fresh chives
- 1½ cups (12 ounces) plus 2 tablespoons heavy cream, measured separately

GATHER COOKING EQUIPMENT

Rimmed baking sheet

Parchment paper

Medium bowl

Whisk

Rubber spatula

Ruler

Bench scraper (or butter knife and spatula)

Pastry brush

Oven mitts

Cooling rack

MAKES 9 biscuits

TOTAL TIME 50 minutes

LEVEL ■■□

"The biscuits tasted like fluffy clouds. I want to make this recipe so many times that I memorize it."
—Cecilia, 8

1 Adjust oven rack to upper-middle position and heat oven to 425 degrees. Line rimmed baking sheet with parchment paper.

2 In medium bowl, whisk together flour, sugar, baking powder, Old Bay, and salt. Add cheddar, Parmesan, and chives to bowl. Use rubber spatula to stir until well combined.

3 Add 1½ cups cream to bowl and stir until no dry flour remains. Lightly sprinkle clean counter with extra flour.

4 Transfer dough to lightly floured counter. Use your hands to gather and press mixture until dough holds together. Shape dough into 9 biscuits following photos, right.

5 Use bench scraper to transfer biscuits to parchment-lined baking sheet, leaving space between biscuits. Use pastry brush to paint tops of biscuits with remaining 2 tablespoons cream.

6 Place baking sheet in oven. Bake until biscuits are golden brown, 14 to 18 minutes.

7 Use oven mitts to remove baking sheet from oven and place on cooling rack (ask an adult for help). Let biscuits cool on baking sheet for 5 minutes. Serve warm.

HOW TO SHAPE BISCUITS

1 Pat dough into 7½-inch square, about ½ inch thick.

2 Use bench scraper to cut dough into 9 equal squares (each square should be about 2½ inches).

THAT'S THE BISCUIT

While we were tempted to pack a whole block of cheese into these biscuits, adding more than ½ cup made the biscuits heavy and greasy from the fat and water in the cheese. To keep our biscuits light and fluffy, we used a combo of extra-sharp cheddar and Parmesan—two cheeses that have a lot of flavor but won't add too much extra moisture to the dough. Old Bay seasoning adds savory, peppery, slightly smoky flavor while oniony minced chives add pops of bright-green color to round out our biscuits.

6 SWEETS

CHOCOLATE SUGAR COOKIES

We developed this recipe with natural unsweetened cocoa powder. If you use Dutch-processed cocoa powder, the cookies will spread more and be more delicate.

PREPARE INGREDIENTS

¾ cup (3¾ ounces) all-purpose flour

⅓ cup (1 ounce) natural unsweetened cocoa powder

¼ teaspoon baking soda

⅛ teaspoon baking powder

¼ teaspoon table salt

¾ cup packed (5¼ ounces) dark brown sugar

6 tablespoons unsalted butter, melted and cooled (see page 12) ▶

1½ teaspoons vanilla extract

1 large egg

¼ cup (1¾ ounces) sugar

GATHER COOKING EQUIPMENT

2 bowls (1 large, 1 medium)

Whisk

Rubber spatula

Rimmed baking sheet

Parchment paper

Shallow dish

Measuring spoons

Sturdy drinking glass or dry measuring cup

Ruler

Oven mitts

Cooling rack

MAKES 12 cookies

TOTAL TIME 1¼ hours, plus cooling time

LEVEL ◼◻◻

"I couldn't wait 30 minutes to taste them, I waited 10 minutes instead. That's the best I could do."
—Blake, 8

1 In medium bowl, whisk together flour, cocoa, baking soda, baking powder, and salt. In large bowl, whisk brown sugar, melted butter, and vanilla until smooth. Add egg and whisk until well combined.

2 Add flour mixture to brown sugar mixture and use rubber spatula to stir until no dry flour is visible and soft dough forms. Let dough sit at room temperature for 30 minutes.

3 Meanwhile, adjust oven rack to middle position and heat oven to 350 degrees. Line rimmed baking sheet with parchment paper.

4 When dough is ready, place sugar in shallow dish. Lightly wet your hands. Use your wet hands to roll dough into 12 balls (about 1 heaping tablespoon each). Place dough balls in dish and roll to coat with sugar.

5 Place sugar-coated dough balls on parchment-lined baking sheet, leaving space between balls. Use bottom of sturdy drinking glass to gently flatten each ball into 2-inch-wide circle (see photo, above right).

6 Scoop 1 teaspoon leftover sugar from dish. Sprinkle cookies evenly with sugar.

7 Place baking sheet in oven. Bake cookies until slightly puffy and edges have begun to set but centers are still soft, 11 to 13 minutes.

8 Use oven mitts to remove baking sheet from oven and place on cooling rack (ask an adult for help). Let cookies cool completely on baking sheet, about 30 minutes. Serve.

HOW TO PRESS COOKIES

Use bottom of sturdy drinking glass (or dry measuring cup) to gently flatten dough balls. This will help them spread evenly in the oven.

GIVE IT A REST

You might be tempted to get straight to rolling your cookie dough into balls instead of letting it rest for 30 minutes, but be patient! Without the rest, you'll be dealing with a soft, sticky mess. This dough contains cocoa powder, which has a hard time absorbing liquid. Giving the dough time to rest allows the starch in the cocoa powder to absorb water from the liquid ingredients. Once the dough is hydrated, it'll be easier to work with, making for a much better cookie-rolling experience.

COWBOY COOKIES

These large cookies need a lot of room to spread out while baking. If you don't have a rimless cookie sheet, you can use a rimmed baking sheet that has been flipped upside down (so that the cookies don't spread into the rimmed edges).

PREPARE INGREDIENTS

¾ cup (3¾ ounces) all-purpose flour

½ teaspoon baking powder

¼ teaspoon baking soda

¼ teaspoon table salt

¾ cup packed (5¼ ounces) light brown sugar

6 tablespoons unsalted butter, melted and cooled (see page 12) ▶

½ teaspoon vanilla extract

1 large egg

⅔ cup (2 ounces) old-fashioned rolled oats

½ cup pecans, chopped coarse

½ cup (1½ ounces) sweetened shredded coconut

⅓ cup (2 ounces) semisweet chocolate chips

Vegetable oil spray

GATHER COOKING EQUIPMENT

Rimless cookie sheet

Parchment paper

2 bowls (1 large, 1 medium)

Whisk

Rubber spatula

¼-cup dry measuring cup

Ruler

Oven mitts

Cooling rack

MAKES 8 cookies

TOTAL TIME 50 minutes, plus cooling time

LEVEL ◼◼◻

"I like how there is a crunchy outside with a yummy gooey middle."
—Lillian, 10

1 Adjust oven rack to middle position and heat oven to 350 degrees. Line rimless cookie sheet with parchment paper.

2 In medium bowl, whisk together flour, baking powder, baking soda, and salt. In large bowl, whisk sugar, melted butter, and vanilla until smooth. Add egg and whisk until well combined.

3 Add flour mixture to sugar mixture and use rubber spatula to stir until no dry flour is visible. Stir in oats, pecans, coconut, and chocolate chips until well combined (mixture will be sticky).

4 Lightly spray ¼-cup dry measuring cup with vegetable oil spray. Use greased measuring cup to scoop 8 portions of dough onto parchment-lined cookie sheet, spacing them about 2½ inches apart (see photo, above right). Respray measuring cup as needed.

5 Lightly spray bottom of measuring cup with vegetable oil spray. Use greased bottom of measuring cup to gently flatten each dough portion into 2½-inch-wide circle (see page 169).

6 Place cookie sheet in oven. Bake cookies until edges are browned and set and centers are puffy but still pale, 15 to 17 minutes.

7 Use oven mitts to remove cookie sheet from oven and place on cooling rack (ask an adult for help). Let cookies cool completely on cookie sheet, about 30 minutes. Serve.

HOW TO STAGGER COOKIES

Cowboy cookies need lots of room to expand and bake evenly (don't fence them in!).

Leave 2½ inches between dough portions, arranging them in staggered rows so that they don't spread into each other as they bake.

TEN-GALLON COOKIES

These supersize cookies—filled with oats, pecans, shredded coconut, and chocolate chips—became popular in the 1950s, thanks to nostalgia for the American cowboy. While cowboys didn't eat these cookies themselves, they get their name because they're hearty enough to keep a hard-working cowboy full. While most cookies are made with 1 or 2 tablespoons of dough each, these cookies use a full ¼ cup—making them double the size of your average cookie! Using a rimless cookie sheet (instead of a rimmed baking sheet) lets the dough spread to full "cowboy size" in the oven.

BROWNIE BITES

Using parchment mini muffin liners instead of paper or foil liners helps prevent the brownie bites from sticking.

PREPARE INGREDIENTS

Vegetable oil spray

3 tablespoons (1⅛ ounces) bittersweet chocolate chips

3 tablespoons (½ ounce) Dutch-processed cocoa powder

¼ cup (2 ounces) water

1 cup (7 ounces) sugar

⅓ cup vegetable oil

1 large egg

1 teaspoon vanilla extract

⅔ cup (3⅓ ounces) all-purpose flour

¼ teaspoon table salt

GATHER COOKING EQUIPMENT

24-cup mini-muffin tin

24 parchment mini muffin liners

Large heatproof bowl

Liquid measuring cup

Oven mitts

Whisk

1-tablespoon measuring spoon

Toothpick

Cooling rack

MAKES 24 brownie bites

TOTAL TIME 50 minutes, plus cooling time

LEVEL ■■□

"So rich and fudgy! My entire family enjoyed them."
—Rishika, 11

START COOKING!

1 Adjust oven rack to middle position and heat oven to 350 degrees. Line 24-cup mini-muffin tin with parchment liners. Generously spray liners in muffin tin with vegetable oil spray. Set aside.

2 In large heatproof bowl, combine chocolate chips and cocoa.

3 Heat water in liquid measuring cup in microwave until hot, 1 to 1½ minutes. Use oven mitts to remove measuring cup from microwave. Pour hot water over chocolate chip mixture and whisk until chocolate is melted and smooth.

4 Whisk in sugar, oil, egg, and vanilla until combined. Whisk in flour and salt until just combined and no dry flour remains.

5 Scoop 1 tablespoon batter into each muffin cup. Evenly divide any remaining batter among cups.

6 Place muffin tin in oven and bake until toothpick inserted in center of 1 brownie bite comes out with few moist crumbs attached, 20 to 23 minutes (see photo, page 15).

7 Use oven mitts to remove muffin tin from oven and place on cooling rack (ask an adult for help). Let brownie bites cool in muffin tin for at least 30 minutes. Serve.

DOUBLE THE CHOCOLATE

To get the most chocolaty flavor, we use two forms of chocolate in this recipe: Dutch-processed cocoa powder and bittersweet chocolate chips. Cocoa powder is made from dry, finely ground bits of cocoa solids that come from roasted cocoa beans. (Yes, chocolate comes from a bean—the fruit of a cacao tree!) We like to use Dutch-processed cocoa powder here because it makes moister brownies with more chocolate flavor than natural cocoa powder. Bittersweet chocolate chips also feature more chocolate flavor than their milk chocolate cousin. Milk chocolate has more dairy and less chocolate than bittersweet chocolate, and it would make these bites too sweet with less chocolate flavor.

BAKING PAN PREP

Following the pan prep steps on these pages prevents your baked goods from sticking, which means that you can easily remove them from the pan.

WHY DO YOU NEED VEGETABLE OIL SPRAY?

To make sure that baked goods don't stick, remember to grease the pan. Rather than using butter or oil, we turn to vegetable oil spray. Giving your pan a spritz covers it in a fine mist, meaning that you get more even coverage.

HOW TO LINE A BAKING PAN WITH PARCHMENT PAPER

To help remove cakes, such as Coconut Snack Cake (page 182), from their pans, we often line the pan with parchment paper before baking. Otherwise, the cake could stick and break into pieces as you attempt to remove it!

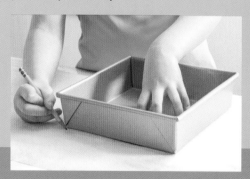

1 Place baking pan on sheet of parchment paper. Use pencil to trace around bottom of pan.

2 Cut out parchment with scissors, following traced line.

HOW TO MAKE AN ALUMINUM FOIL SLING ▶

Lining a baking pan with two pieces of aluminum foil makes it supereasy to get baked goods, such as Berry Streusel Bars (page 176), out of the pan. For an 8-inch square pan, both sheets of foil should measure 8 inches wide and roughly 13 inches long.

1 Fold 2 long sheets of aluminum foil to match width of baking pan. Both sheets should be same width for square pans.

2 Lay sheets of foil in pan so sheets are perpendicular to each other. Let extra foil hang over edges of pan. Push foil into corners and up sides of pan, smoothing foil so it rests against pan.

HOW TO PORTION BATTER FOR MUFFINS AND CUPCAKES

In recipes for muffins and cupcakes, you scoop batter into the individual cups of a muffin tin using a dry measuring cup or a measuring spoon.

Use rubber spatula to help you push and scrape sticky batter out of measuring cup or spoon.

VIDEO

▶ Making a foil sling

BERRY STREUSEL BARS

You can use frozen berries in this recipe, if you like—make sure to thaw them before using.

PREPARE INGREDIENTS

CRUST

Vegetable oil spray

1¼ cups (6¼ ounces) all-purpose flour

⅓ cup (2⅓ ounces) sugar

¼ teaspoon table salt

8 tablespoons unsalted butter, cut into 8 pieces and chilled

STREUSEL AND FILLING

¼ cup (¾ ounce) old-fashioned rolled oats

2 tablespoons packed brown sugar

1 tablespoon unsalted butter, cut into 4 pieces and softened (see page 12) ▶

½ cup (2½ ounces) raspberries, blueberries, or strawberries (strawberries hulled and chopped)

½ cup raspberry, blueberry, or strawberry jam

1 teaspoon lemon juice, squeezed from ½ lemon (see page 14) ▶

Pinch table salt

MAKES **16 bars**

TOTAL TIME **1½ hours, plus 2 hours cooling time**

LEVEL ◼◼◻

"It was delicious! I liked the crumbly topping with the sweet fruit inside."
—Serenity, 12

GATHER COOKING EQUIPMENT

Aluminum foil

8-inch square metal baking pan

Ruler

Food processor

½-cup dry measuring cup

Medium bowl

Rubber spatula

Oven mitts

Cooling rack

Cutting board

Chef's knife

A TASTY TRIO

These bars have three distinct layers that combine into one "berry" delicious treat. The cookie-like crust is sturdy enough to support the other layers; the jammy filling is fruity, but not too sweet thanks to a bit of tart lemon juice; and the streusel topping is buttery and tender. The word streusel ("STREW-sul") comes from the German word streuen ("SHTROY-en") meaning "to sprinkle" or "to scatter." You'll find this crumbly mixture of flour, sugar, butter (and sometimes spices, nuts, and oats) topping all sorts of baked goods, from fruit desserts to muffins to cakes. In these bars, it's the perfect complement to the fruity filling.

START COOKING!

1. **For the crust:** Adjust oven rack to middle position and heat oven to 375 degrees. Make aluminum foil sling for 8-inch square metal baking pan (see photos, page 175). Spray foil with vegetable oil spray. ▶

2. Add flour, sugar, and salt to food processor and lock lid into place. Turn on processor and process until combined, about 5 seconds. Stop processor.

3. Remove lid, add 8 tablespoons chilled butter to processor, and lock lid back into place. Hold down pulse button for 1 second, then release. Repeat until butter is combined with flour mixture and looks like wet sand, about twenty 1-second pulses.

4. Remove lid and carefully remove processor blade (ask an adult for help). Scoop ½ cup dough mixture into medium bowl; set aside for streusel topping. Use rubber spatula to scrape remaining mixture into greased foil-lined baking pan.

5. Use your hands to press mixture into even layer covering bottom of baking pan. Use bottom of ½-cup dry measuring cup to press mixture firmly into pan until very flat.

6. Place baking pan in oven. Bake until crust begins to brown at edges, 15 to 18 minutes.

KEEP GOING! →

HOW TO MAKE STREUSEL TOPPING

1 Rub mixture between your fingers until butter is fully incorporated and mixture clumps together.

2 Use your fingers to pinch oat mixture into small clumps and sprinkle evenly over filling.

7 Use oven mitts to remove baking pan from oven and place on cooling rack (ask an adult for help). Let crust cool for at least 15 minutes. (Do not turn off oven.)

8 **For the streusel and filling:** While crust cools, add oats and brown sugar to bowl with reserved dough mixture from step 4. Use rubber spatula to stir until combined.

9 Add 1 tablespoon softened butter to oat mixture and rub mixture between your fingers until butter is fully incorporated and mixture clumps together (see photo 1, above).

10 Add raspberries, jam, lemon juice, and salt to now-empty food processor and lock lid into place. Hold down pulse button for 1 second, then release. Repeat until raspberries are broken down, about five 1-second pulses.

11 Remove lid and carefully remove processor blade (ask an adult for help). Pour raspberry mixture over cooled crust, using rubber spatula to scrape out all filling from processor bowl. Spread filling into even layer.

12 Use your fingers to pinch oat mixture into small clumps and sprinkle evenly over filling (see photo 2, above).

13 Place baking pan in oven and bake until filling is bubbling and topping is golden brown, 24 to 28 minutes.

14 Use oven mitts to remove baking pan from oven and place on cooling rack (ask an adult for help). Let bars cool completely in pan, about 2 hours.

15 Use foil to lift bars out of baking pan and transfer to cutting board. Use chef's knife tut into squares. Serve.

PEANUT BUTTER–CHOCOLATE TORTILLA TRIANGLES

PREPARE INGREDIENTS

2 (8-inch) flour tortillas

2 tablespoons creamy or chunky peanut butter

2 tablespoons chocolate chips

1 tablespoon unsalted butter, melted and cooled (see page 12) ▶

1–2 teaspoons confectioners' (powdered) sugar

GATHER COOKING EQUIPMENT

Cutting board

Butter knife

Pastry brush

10-inch nonstick skillet

Spatula

Chef's knife

Fine-mesh strainer

Small bowl

SERVES 2

TOTAL TIME 20 minutes

LEVEL ■■☐☐

"They had a perfect balance of peanut butter and chocolate on the inside. So good! I made them twice."
—Gia, 13

START COOKING!

1 Place tortillas on cutting board. Use butter knife to spread peanut butter over half of each tortilla, leaving border around edge. Sprinkle chocolate chips evenly over peanut butter. Fold tortillas in half, forming half-moon shape, and press to flatten.

2 Use pastry brush to paint top of each folded tortilla with half of melted butter. Place tortillas in 10-inch nonstick skillet, buttered sides down. Paint second side of each tortilla with remaining butter.

3 Cook over medium heat until bottoms of tortillas are crisp and browned, 3 to 6 minutes.

4 Use spatula to flip tortillas. Cook until second sides are crisp and browned, 1 to 2 minutes. Turn off heat.

5 Slide tortillas out of skillet and onto cutting board. Let cool for 2 minutes. Use chef's knife to cut each tortilla in half. Dust tortilla triangles with confectioners' sugar following photos, right. Serve warm.

HOW TO DUST WITH CONFECTIONERS' SUGAR

1 Set fine-mesh strainer over small bowl. Add confectioners' sugar to strainer.

2 Use fine-mesh strainer to dust confectioners' sugar evenly over triangles, gently tapping side of strainer to release sugar.

PB AND C, PLEASE!

Move over, PB and J, there's a new combination in town! Peanut butter and chocolate are made to be together—the melty chocolate and peanut butter create a sweet and salty combination that never disappoints. The chocolate chips melt and mix with the peanut butter to create a gooey filling, and the toasted tortillas get crispy on the outside as they cook. Bonus: This recipe is quick to make, and it makes just enough to share with a sibling or friend.

COCONUT SNACK CAKE

Cream of coconut is often found in the soda and drink-mix aisle of the grocery store. Be sure to shake it well before measuring because it separates as it stands. Do not use coconut cream in this recipe.

PREPARE INGREDIENTS

Vegetable oil spray

1½ cups (7½ ounces) all-purpose flour

1½ teaspoons baking powder

¾ teaspoon table salt

1¼ cups cream of coconut (see note above)

½ cup (4 ounces) whole milk

2 large eggs

3 tablespoons unsalted butter, melted and cooled (see page 12)

1½ teaspoons vanilla extract

½ teaspoon coconut extract

½ cup (1½ ounces) sweetened shredded coconut

1–2 teaspoons confectioners' (powdered) sugar

GATHER COOKING EQUIPMENT

8-inch square metal baking pan

8-inch square piece of parchment paper (see page 174)

3 bowls (1 large, 1 medium, 1 small)

Whisk

Rubber spatula

Toothpick

Oven mitts

Cooling rack

Butter knife

Fine-mesh strainer

Cutting board

Chef's knife

SERVES 12

TOTAL TIME 1¼ hours, plus 2 hours cooling time

LEVEL

"This was very coconutty and easy to make. It tasted really good!"
—Vivian, 11

1 Adjust oven rack to middle position and heat oven to 325 degrees. Spray inside bottom and sides of 8-inch square metal baking pan with vegetable oil spray. Line bottom of baking pan with 8-inch square piece of parchment paper.

2 In medium bowl, whisk together flour, baking powder, and salt. In large bowl, whisk together cream of coconut, milk, eggs, melted butter, vanilla, and coconut extract.

3 Add flour mixture to cream of coconut mixture and whisk until just combined and no dry flour remains. Use rubber spatula to stir in shredded coconut.

4 Scrape batter into parchment-lined baking pan and smooth top (make sure to spread batter into corners to create even layer).

5 Place baking pan in oven. Bake until toothpick inserted in center of cake comes out clean (see photo, page 15), 35 to 45 minutes.

6 Use oven mitts to remove baking pan from oven and place on cooling rack (ask an adult for help). Let cake cool completely in pan, about 2 hours.

7 Remove cake from baking pan and discard parchment following photo, above right. Dust cake with confectioners' sugar (see photos, page 181). Transfer cake to cutting board, use chef's knife to cut cake into pieces, and serve.

HOW TO REMOVE CAKES FROM PANS

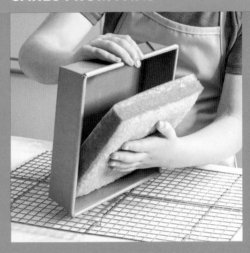

Run butter knife around edge of cake to release cake from pan. Gently flip cake out of pan, peel parchment paper away from cake, and discard parchment.

A WHOLE LOT OF COCONUT

Three different coconut products give this cake lots of coconut flavor and just the right amount of sweetness. The coconut extract boosts the cake's tropical taste, and mixing sweetened shredded coconut into the batter results in a cake studded with sweet, slightly chewy bits of coconut. Cream of coconut contains a lot of sugar, so it (and the sweetened shredded coconut) add plenty of sweetness—enough that you don't need to add any granulated sugar to this cake! Just don't confuse sweet cream of coconut with unsweetened coconut cream—that's a different product.

RED VELVET CUPCAKES

Do not substitute Dutch-processed cocoa powder for natural unsweetened cocoa powder here; the natural cocoa helps turn the cake red. We prefer liquid food coloring to gel or paste colors for this recipe, as it's much easier to mix together with the cocoa.

PREPARE INGREDIENTS

- 1 cup plus 2 tablespoons (5⅔ ounces) all-purpose flour
- ¾ teaspoon baking soda
-    Pinch table salt
- ½ cup (4 ounces) buttermilk
- 1 large egg
- 1½ teaspoons distilled white vinegar
- 1½ teaspoons vanilla extract
- 1 tablespoon natural unsweetened cocoa powder
- 1 tablespoon red food coloring
- 6 tablespoons unsalted butter, cut into 6 pieces and softened (see page 12) ▶
- ¾ cup (5¼ ounces) sugar
- 3 cups Cream Cheese Frosting (see page 187)

MAKES 12 cupcakes

TOTAL TIME 1¼ hours, plus 1¼ hours cooling time

LEVEL ◼◼◻

"The cupcake was moist and delicious!"
—Micah, 8

GATHER COOKING EQUIPMENT

12-cup muffin tin	Rubber spatula
12 paper cupcake liners	1-tablespoon measuring spoon
3 bowls (2 medium, 1 small)	Toothpick
Whisk	Oven mitts
Spoon	Cooling rack
Electric mixer (stand mixer with paddle attachment or handheld mixer and large bowl)	Small icing (offset) spatula or spoon

START COOKING!

1   Adjust oven rack to middle position and heat oven to 350 degrees. Line 12-cup muffin tin with paper liners.

2   In medium bowl, whisk together flour, baking soda, and salt. In second medium bowl, whisk together buttermilk, egg, vinegar, and vanilla. In small bowl, use spoon to mix cocoa and food coloring until smooth paste forms.

3   In bowl of stand mixer (or large bowl if using handheld mixer), combine softened butter and sugar. If using stand mixer, lock bowl into place and attach paddle to stand mixer. Start mixer on medium speed and beat until mixture is pale and fluffy, about 3 minutes. Stop mixer.

KEEP GOING!

HOW RED VELVET CUPCAKES GET THEIR COLOR

To give these cupcakes their brilliant red color, we use some cakey chemistry. Cocoa powder contains molecules called anthocyanins ("ann-though-SIGH-ah-nins"). When anthocyanins interact with acids—in this recipe, buttermilk and vinegar—they turn red (don't worry, you won't taste the vinegar!). That chemical reaction produces a faint red color in these cupcakes—pretty, but we wanted them to live up to their colorful name! To boost their red hue, we also add a full tablespoon of red food coloring. Mixing the food coloring and cocoa powder into a paste helps distribute the cocoa evenly in the batter, creating a more even red color. And remember, these aren't chocolate cupcakes! The little bit of cocoa powder is there for color.

4   Use rubber spatula to scrape down sides of bowl. Carefully add half of flour mixture. Start mixer on low speed and mix until just combined, about 30 seconds. With mixer running, add buttermilk mixture and mix until combined, about 30 seconds. Stop mixer.

5   Scrape down sides of bowl. Add remaining flour mixture. Start mixer on low speed and mix until no dry flour remains, 30 seconds to 1 minute. Stop mixer.

6   Add cocoa mixture. Start mixer and mix on low speed until color is evenly distributed, about 30 seconds. Stop mixer. Remove bowl from stand mixer, if using. Scrape down sides of bowl and stir in any remaining dry flour.

7   Divide batter evenly between muffin cups (about 2 tablespoons each).

8   Place muffin tin in oven. Bake until toothpick inserted in center of 1 cupcake comes out clean (see photo, page 15), 15 to 20 minutes.

9   Use oven mitts to remove muffin tin from oven and place on cooling rack (ask an adult for help). Let cupcakes cool in muffin tin for 15 minutes.

10 Remove cupcakes from muffin tin and transfer directly to cooling rack. Let cupcakes cool completely, about 1 hour. (This is a good time to make the frosting!)

11 Use small icing (offset) spatula to spread 2 to 3 tablespoons Cream Cheese Frosting over each cupcake (see photos, above right). Serve.

HOW TO FROST CUPCAKES

1 Mound 2 to 3 tablespoons frosting in center of cupcake.

2 Use icing (offset) spatula to spread frosting to edge of cupcake, leaving slight mound of frosting in center. Keep frosting off paper liner.

CREAM CHEESE FROSTING

MAKES 3 cups

TOTAL TIME 20 minutes

DIFFICULTY ▬ ■ ■

PREPARE INGREDIENTS

12	ounces cream cheese, softened
6	tablespoons unsalted butter, cut into 6 pieces and softened (see page 12) ▶
1½	tablespoons sour cream
1	teaspoon vanilla extract
⅛	teaspoon table salt
1½	cups (6 ounces) confectioners' (powdered) sugar

GATHER COOKING EQUIPMENT

Electric mixer (stand mixer with paddle attachment or handheld mixer and large bowl)

Rubber spatula

1   In bowl of stand mixer (or large bowl if using handheld mixer), combine softened cream cheese, softened butter, sour cream, vanilla, and salt. Lock bowl into place and attach paddle to stand mixer, if using.

2   Start mixer on medium speed and beat until smooth, about 1 minute. Stop mixer. Use rubber spatula to scrape down sides of bowl.

3   Start mixer on low speed. Slowly add sugar, a little bit at a time, and beat until smooth, about 4 minutes.

4   Increase speed to medium-high and beat until frosting is light and fluffy, about 5 minutes. Stop mixer. Remove bowl from stand mixer, if using.

MEASURING INGREDIENTS

It's important to measure accurately, especially when you're baking. There are two ways to measure: by volume and by weight.

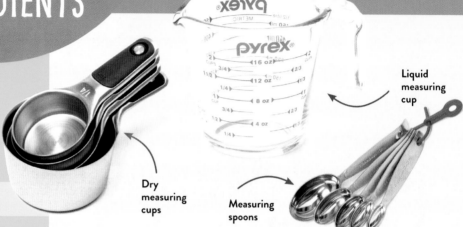

Liquid measuring cup

Dry measuring cups

Measuring spoons

VIDEOS

Measuring liquid ingredients

Measuring dry ingredients

Using a scale

HOW TO MEASURE LIQUID INGREDIENTS BY VOLUME ▶

Liquid ingredients (such as milk, water, or juice) should be measured in a liquid measuring cup (a clear plastic or glass cup with lines on the side, a big handle, and a pour spout).

Place the measuring cup on the counter and bend down to read the bottom of the concave arc at the liquid's surface. This is known as the meniscus line.

HOW TO MEASURE DRY INGREDIENTS BY VOLUME ▶

Dry ingredients should be measured with dry measuring cups—small metal or plastic cups with handles. Each set has cups of various sizes—¼ cup, ⅓ cup, ½ cup, and 1 cup are standard.

Dip the measuring cup into the ingredient and sweep away the excess with the back of a butter knife.

SMALL AMOUNTS REQUIRE SMALL TOOLS

Use measuring spoons for small amounts of liquid and dry ingredients. For dry ingredients, remember to sweep away the excess with the back of a butter knife.

KITCHEN MATH

3 teaspoons	=	1 tablespoon
16 tablespoons	=	1 cup
2 cups	=	1 pint
2 pints	=	1 quart
4 quarts	=	1 gallon
16 ounces	=	1 pound

HOW TO MEASURE BY WEIGHT USING A SCALE ▶

Using a scale is the most accurate way to measure dry and liquid ingredients, if you have one.

1 Turn on the scale and place the bowl on the scale. Then press the "tare" button to zero out the weight (that means that the weight of the bowl won't be included!).

2 Slowly add your ingredient to the bowl until you reach the desired weight. Here we are weighing 5 ounces of all-purpose flour (equal to 1 cup).

SKILLET STONE FRUIT CRISP

PREPARE INGREDIENTS

TOPPING

¼ cup plus ½ cup sliced almonds, measured separately

⅔ cup (3⅓ ounces) all-purpose flour

½ cup packed (3½ ounces) light brown sugar

½ teaspoon vanilla extract

¼ teaspoon table salt

¼ teaspoon ground cinnamon

6 tablespoons unsalted butter, cut into 6 pieces

FILLING

¼ cup (1¾ ounces) sugar

1½ teaspoons cornstarch

2 pounds ripe peaches, nectarines, or plums, pitted and cut into ½-inch-thick wedges

1 tablespoon lemon juice, squeezed from ½ lemon (see page 14) ▶

Pinch ground nutmeg

Pinch ground cinnamon

GATHER COOKING EQUIPMENT

Cutting board	Plate
Chef's knife	Whisk
2 bowls (1 large, 1 medium)	Paper towels
	Oven mitts
Rubber spatula	
10-inch nonstick skillet with lid	

SERVES 6

TOTAL TIME 1 hour

LEVEL

"I liked the crunchiness of the crisp next to the sweetness and softness of the peaches."
—Isadora, 10

START COOKING!

1   **For the topping:** Place ¼ cup almonds on cutting board and use chef's knife to chop fine. In medium bowl, combine flour, brown sugar, vanilla, salt, ¼ teaspoon cinnamon, chopped almonds, and remaining ½ cup sliced almonds. Use rubber spatula to stir until evenly combined.

2   In 10-inch nonstick skillet, melt butter over medium heat. Add almond mixture and stir until well combined and no dry flour remains. Cook, stirring and scraping bottom of skillet often, until almonds begin to brown, 4 to 6 minutes.

3   Turn off heat and slide skillet to cool burner. Use rubber spatula to scrape almond mixture onto plate (ask an adult for help). Set aside topping to cool.

4   **For the filling:** In large bowl, whisk together sugar and cornstarch. Add peaches, lemon juice, nutmeg, and pinch cinnamon, and use clean rubber spatula to toss gently to combine.

5   Use paper towels to carefully wipe out now-empty skillet (skillet will be warm). Add peach mixture to skillet and cover with lid. Cook over medium heat until peaches release their juice, 5 to 10 minutes. (If skillet looks dry and fruit has not yet released juice after 10 minutes, add ¼ cup water to skillet.)

6   Use oven mitts to remove lid. Reduce heat to medium-low and continue to cook, stirring occasionally, until peaches are soft and sauce thickens, 5 to 10 minutes. Turn off heat and slide skillet to cool burner.

7   Sprinkle cooled topping evenly over peaches, breaking up any large chunks with your hands. Let crisp cool slightly, about 10 minutes. Serve.

WHO NEEDS THE OVEN?

A summery fruit dessert, no oven required? Yes, please! Though a traditional fruit crisp is usually baked, we make this version on the stovetop by preparing the topping and filling separately. First, we cook the topping and transfer it to a plate, and then we use that same skillet to cook the fruit filling. As the fruit cooks, it releases its (delicious) juices. But since we don't want a watery crisp, we keep on cooking until the juices reduce, leaving behind a syrupy sauce surrounding pieces of tender fruit. Sprinkle on your already-cooked topping, and serve this dessert straight from the skillet!

LIME POSSET

PREPARE INGREDIENTS

2 cups heavy cream

⅔ cup sugar

1 tablespoon grated lime zest plus
6 tablespoons lime juice, zested and
squeezed from 3 limes (see page 14)

1½ cups (7½ ounces) raspberries
and/or blueberries

GATHER COOKING EQUIPMENT

Large saucepan

Rubber spatula

4-cup liquid measuring cup

Fine-mesh strainer

6 (4-ounce) ramekins or jars

> "The Lime Posset
> was tangy and
> creamy. It made my
> mouth feel happy!"
> —Sebastian, 12

SERVES 6

TOTAL TIME 45 minutes, plus 3 hours
chilling time

LEVEL ◼◻◻

1. In large saucepan, use rubber spatula to stir cream, sugar, and lime zest until well combined. Bring cream mixture to boil over medium heat, stirring often. Cook mixture for 5 minutes, stirring often (mixture will bubble up higher in saucepan towards end of cooking).

2. Turn off heat and slide saucepan to cool burner. Pour cream mixture into liquid measuring cup (ask an adult for help—saucepan and mixture will be VERY hot). Mixture should measure 2 cups. If it is more than 2 cups, return mixture to saucepan and continue to cook over medium-low heat until mixture measures 2 cups, 1 to 2 more minutes.

3. Pour mixture back into saucepan and stir in lime juice. Let mixture cool for 20 minutes.

4. Set fine-mesh strainer over clean liquid measuring cup. Pour mixture through strainer into measuring cup. Discard solids in strainer.

5. Divide mixture evenly among six 4-ounce ramekins. Place in refrigerator, uncovered, and chill until firm, at least 3 hours. Top lime possets with berries and serve. (Once chilled, lime possets can be wrapped in plastic wrap and refrigerated for up to 2 days. Unwrap and let sit at room temperature for 10 minutes before serving.)

POSSET'S MAIN SQUEEZE

Most puddings and custards get their smooth, solid-but-scoopable texture by adding special thickening ingredients such as flour, cornstarch, gelatin, or egg yolks to hot cream (see Banana Cream Pie in a Jar, page 194). But with posset, you just need an acid (such as lime juice) and heavy cream to achieve that texture. When you add acidic lime juice to cream, it causes some of the tiny protein molecules in the cream to bond together in a net, trapping the liquid and creating a thicker texture. At the same time, fat molecules in the cream keep our posset's protein net loose, resulting in a smooth, creamy (but not chunky!) dessert.

BANANA CREAM PIE IN A JAR

PREPARE INGREDIENTS

- 2 ripe bananas
- 5 tablespoons sugar
- 3 large egg yolks (see page 37)
- 1 tablespoon cornstarch
- ⅛ teaspoon table salt
- 1¼ cups half-and-half
- 2 tablespoons unsalted butter
- ½ teaspoon vanilla extract
- 2 whole graham crackers, broken into pieces (or ⅓ cup store-bought graham cracker crumbs)
- 1 recipe Whipped Cream (see page 196)

GATHER COOKING EQUIPMENT

Cutting board	Liquid measuring cup
Chef's knife	Fine-mesh strainer
Ruler	Plastic wrap
2 bowls (1 large, 1 medium)	Large zipper-lock plastic bag
Whisk	Rolling pin
Medium saucepan	1-tablespoon measuring spoon
Rubber spatula	4 (4-ounce) jars or small drinking glasses
Dish towel	
Ladle	

SERVES 4

TOTAL TIME 40 minutes, plus 1 hour chilling time

LEVEL ▪▪◻

"I liked it! I learned a lot about tempering."
—Adia, 11

START COOKING!

1 Peel 1 banana and place on cutting board. Use chef's knife to slice banana into ½-inch-thick circles.

2 In large bowl, whisk sugar, egg yolks, cornstarch, and salt until smooth and pale yellow, about 1 minute.

3 In medium saucepan, combine half-and-half and sliced banana. Place saucepan over medium heat and cook, stirring occasionally with rubber spatula, until mixture comes to simmer, 5 to 7 minutes (small bubbles should break often across surface of mixture). Turn off heat.

4 Place bowl with egg yolk mixture on top of damp dish towel. Temper custard following photos, right.

5 Place fine-mesh strainer over medium bowl. Use rubber spatula to scrape custard into fine-mesh strainer (ask an adult for help—saucepan will be heavy and hot). Gently stir and press custard through strainer (do not try to force banana pieces through strainer). Discard solids in strainer.

6 Add butter and vanilla to custard and whisk until butter is melted. Press sheet of plastic wrap directly onto surface of custard. Place bowl in refrigerator and chill for at least 1 hour and up to 24 hours.

HOW TO TEMPER CUSTARD

1 Use ladle to measure ½ cup hot half-and-half mixture into liquid measuring cup (ask an adult for help). Slowly pour into egg yolk mixture, whisking constantly (the towel will keep the bowl steady).

2 Pour warm egg yolk mixture back into saucepan with half-and-half mixture. Return saucepan to medium heat and cook, using rubber spatula to stir gently but constantly, until mixture begins to bubble and is thickened and pudding-like, about 2 minutes. Turn off heat and carefully slide saucepan to cool burner.

7   When custard is chilled, place cracker pieces in large zipper-lock plastic bag. Press out as much air as possible from bag and seal bag. Use rolling pin to gently crush graham crackers into crumbs. Place 1 tablespoon crumbs in bottom of each jar.

8   Peel remaining banana. Slice banana into ½-inch-thick circles. Use clean rubber spatula to divide chilled custard evenly among jars. Top each jar with whipped cream, banana slices, and remaining graham cracker crumbs, dividing evenly. Serve.

CREAMY CUSTARD 101

For a rich, smooth, and creamy custard, we turned to these three tips. First, we use a technique called tempering to slowly warm up the egg yolks so that they thicken the custard but don't turn into scrambled eggs (see page 97 to learn more about tempering). Then, we constantly stir the custard as it finishes cooking and press it through a strainer to catch any solid bits. Finally, pressing plastic wrap directly onto the surface of the custard prevents a solid "skin" from forming as it chills.

WHIPPED CREAM

For great whipped cream, heavy or whipping cream is a must—and make sure that the cream is cold. Use an electric mixer for the fastest results, although you can use a whisk and whip cream by hand—just be prepared for a workout! If using a mixer, keep the beaters low in the bowl to minimize splatters. This recipe makes about 1 cup. (To make 2 cups, double all ingredients.)

To make whipped cream:

In large bowl, combine ½ cup chilled heavy cream, 1½ teaspoons sugar, and ½ teaspoon vanilla extract. Use electric mixer on medium-low speed to whip cream for 1 minute. Increase speed to high and whip until cream is smooth and thick, about 1 minute. Stop mixer and lift beaters out of cream. If cream clings to beaters and makes soft peaks that stand up on their own, you're done. If not, keep beating and check again in 30 seconds. Don't overwhip cream.

GAJAR KA HALWA (INDIAN CARROT PUDDING)

Ghee is a type of clarified butter used often in Indian cooking. You can find it in the Indian section of most supermarkets, or in the baking aisle near the cooking oils or shortening.

PREPARE INGREDIENTS

¼ cup ghee

1 pound carrots, peeled and grated (see photo, right)

1 teaspoon ground cardamom

3 cups whole milk

⅓ cup sugar

¼ cup chopped cashews

2 tablespoons golden raisins

2 tablespoons finely chopped pistachios (optional)

GATHER COOKING EQUIPMENT

12-inch nonstick skillet

Rubber spatula

SERVES 4

TOTAL TIME 1¼ hours

LEVEL ■■□

1 In 12-inch nonstick skillet, melt ghee over medium heat. Add grated carrots and use rubber spatula to stir until carrots are evenly coated with ghee. Cook, stirring occasionally, until softened, about 10 minutes.

2 Stir in cardamom and cook for 30 seconds. Add milk and bring mixture to simmer (small bubbles should break often across surface of mixture).

3 Reduce heat to medium-low and cook, stirring occasionally, until carrots are very soft and mixture has texture of loose oatmeal, 25 to 30 minutes.

4 Stir in sugar, cashews, and raisins. Cook, stirring often, until mixture is thickened and spatula leaves clear trail through carrot mixture, 8 to 10 minutes. Turn off heat and slide skillet to cool burner.

5 Let pudding cool in skillet for at least 10 minutes. Serve warm or at room temperature, sprinkling individual portions with pistachios (if using).

"At first we weren't sure how pudding from carrots and nuts was going to taste, but it was good."
—Michael, 11 & Isabella, 9

HOW TO GRATE CARROTS

There are two ways to grate carrots: on the large holes of a box grater, or with a food processor. The fastest and easiest way to grate a pound of carrots is to use a food processor.

Ask an adult to set up food processor with shredding disk. Use chef's knife to cut peeled carrots into sections the same length as processor's feed tube. Place carrot in tube. Turn on processor. Then, use plunger to guide carrot into machine.

EAT YOUR VEGETABLES (FOR DESSERT!)

Halwa ("hall-VAH") is a pudding-like sweet popular throughout India that's made from grains, fruits, or vegetables cooked in milk and sugar until soft, sticky, and spoonable. Gajar ka halwa ("GAH-juh kah hall-VAH") is made with carrots ("gajar" means "carrot" in Hindi) and is especially popular in the wintertime when a type of extra-sweet red carrot is available in India (though you can make gajar ka halwa with any color of carrot, in any season you like!). Dressed up with cardamom, nuts, and dried fruit, gajar ka halwa is a sweet way to enjoy your vegetables.

CONVERSIONS & EQUIVALENTS

The recipes in this book were developed using standard U.S. measures. The charts below offer equivalents for U.S. and metric measures. All conversions are approximate and have been rounded up or down to the nearest whole number.

VOLUME CONVERSIONS

U.S.	METRIC
1 teaspoon	5 milliliters
2 teaspoons	10 milliliters
1 tablespoon	15 milliliters
2 tablespoons	30 milliliters
¼ cup	59 milliliters
⅓ cup	79 milliliters
½ cup	118 milliliters
¾ cup	177 milliliters
1 cup	237 milliliters
2 cups (1 pint)	473 milliliters
4 cups (1 quart)	946 milliliters
4 quarts (1 gallon)	3.8 liters

WEIGHT CONVERSIONS

U.S.	METRIC
½ ounce	14 grams
¾ ounce	21 grams
1 ounce	28 grams
2 ounces	57 grams
3 ounces	85 grams
4 ounces	113 grams
5 ounces	142 grams
6 ounces	170 grams
8 ounces	227 grams
10 ounces	283 grams
12 ounces	340 grams
16 ounces (1 pound)	454 grams

OVEN TEMPERATURES

FAHRENHEIT	CELSIUS	GAS MARK
225°	105°	¼
250°	120°	½
275°	135°	1
300°	150°	2
325°	165°	3
350°	180°	4
375°	190°	5
400°	200°	6
425°	220°	7
450°	230°	8
475°	245°	9

CONVERTING TEMPERATURES FROM AN INSTANT-READ THERMOMETER

We include doneness temperatures in some recipes in this book. We recommend an instant-read thermometer for the job. To convert a temperature from Fahrenheit to Celsius, subtract 32 from the Fahrenheit reading, and then divide the result by 1.8.

Example
"Roast chicken until thighs register 175°F."

To Convert
175°F – 32 = 143°
143° ÷ 1.8 = 79.44°C, rounded down to 79°C

RECIPE STATS

	Per Serving	Calories	Fat (g)	Saturated Fat (g)	Sodium (mg)	Carbohy-drates (g)	Fiber (g)	Total Sugar (g)	Added Sugar (g)	Protein (g)
CHAPTER 1 - BREAKFAST										
Pumpkin Muffins	Per muffin	320	15	1.5	380	44	0	28	26	3
Buttermilk Pancakes	Serves 2–4	300	11	7	380	40	0	7	3	9
Waffles	Serves 2–4	470	16	9	1260	64	0	11	6	13
Apple-Cinnamon Syrup	Per 2 tablespoons	100	0	0	25	27	0	24	21	0
Butter-Pecan Syrup	Per 2 tablespoons	110	4	1	20	21	0	18	18	0
Chocolate Pastry Puffs	Per pastry	250	16	8	150	28	2	1	0	5
Cinnamon-Raisin Swirl Bread	Serves 10	380	9	1	410	67	0	35	27	7
Breakfast Quesadillas	Serves 4	530	36	12	1060	32	1	2	0	22
Fancy Scrambled Eggs	Serves 2	200	16	8	190	2	0	1	0	11
Eggs in a Hole	Serves 2	240	12	5	370	22	0	3	0	9
Breakfast Cookies	Per cookie	170	7	2	105	23	2	10	8	4
Apricot-Pepita Breakfast Cookies	Per cookie	170	7	2	105	23	2	11	8	4
Raisin–Sunflower Seed Breakfast Cookies	Per cookie	180	7	2	110	24	2	11	8	4
Blueberry Baked Oatmeal	Serves 8	350	13	7	450	51	4	29	24	7
CHAPTER 2 - SNACKS										
Chili-Lime Tropical Trail Mix	Per ¼ cup	190	14	3.5	135	13	3	8	1	5
Garlic-Sesame Nori Chips	Serves 2–4	50	4.5	0.5	120	1	1	0	0	1
Watermelon-Mango Skewers with Tajín	Serves 4	70	0	0	330	17	1	14	1	1
Edamame with Lemon-Pepper Salt	Serves 4	90	4	0	850	7	4	2	0	10
Edamame with Sriracha-Lime Salt	Serves 4	90	4	0	870	7	4	2	0	10
Caramelized Onion Dip	Per ¼ cup	100	8	3.5	250	7	1	4	0	1
Loaded Nachos	Serves 8	240	14	6	390	16	1	1	0	13
Cheesy Breadsticks	Serves 4–6	220	9	4.5	550	26	1	1	1	8
Baked Brie	Serves 6	170	10	7	240	12	0	8	0	8
Rosemary Socca (Chickpea Flour Pancakes)	Serves 2	280	17	2	590	26	7	4	0	9

Per Serving		Calories	Fat (g)	Saturated Fat (g)	Sodium (mg)	Carbohy-drates (g)	Fiber (g)	Total Sugar (g)	Added Sugar (g)	Protein (g)
CHAPTER 3 - LUNCH										
Chicken Caesar Salad Wraps	Serves 2	510	27	6	1040	37	1	3	0	31
Turkey and Cheddar Sandwiches with Pickled Apple	Serves 2	670	32	14	1590	64	3	39	25	31
Open-Faced Tuna Melts	Serves 2	460	27	10	1190	25	1	5	0	29
Wedge Salads with Ranch Dressing	Serves 4	230	21	5	360	6	2	4	0	5
Pita "Pizzas" with Hummus, Feta, and Tomatoes	Serves 2	520	29	11	1110	43	1	4	0	22
Cucumber-Avocado Maki	Serves 2–4	400	8	1	570	75	5	4	2	8
Creamy Secret Ingredient Pasta	Serves 2	390	8	2.5	280	63	3	2	0	16
Kimchi-Miso Ramen	Serves 2	420	9	0.5	2020	66	5	5	0	20
Spiced Red Lentil Soup	Serves 4	430	16	9	1200	53	9	3	0	20
CHAPTER 4 - DINNER										
Pan-Seared Chicken Breasts with Garlic-Herb Sauce	Serves 4	350	19	8	390	2	0	1	0	39
Oven-Baked Chicken with Teriyaki Sauce	Serves 4	230	7	2	770	5	0	5	4	35
Avgolemono Soup (Greek Chicken and Rice Soup with Egg and Lemon)	Serves 4–6	270	6	1.5	1410	26	0	1	0	26
Slow-Roasted Salmon	Serves 4–6	330	21	4	310	2	0	2	1	32
Fish Tacos with Creamy Cilantro Sauce	Serves 4	340	17	3.5	740	28	2	1	0	19
Honey-Mustard Pork Chops	Serves 4	370	14	6	830	19	1	11	10	40
Sizzling Beef Lettuce Wraps	Serves 4	420	31	9	900	11	1	8	7	24
Quick Pickled Cucumbers	Serves 8	15	0	0	75	3	0	3	2	0
Oven-Baked Spaghetti and Meatballs	Serves 4	480	16	6	850	56	2	8	0	26
Pasta with Kale-Basil Pesto	Serves 4–6	500	25	3.5	380	56	3	2	0	12
One-Pot Garlicky Shrimp Pasta	Serves 4	490	13	2	1730	65	3	2	0	27
Instant Mashed Potato Gnocchi with Browned Butter Sauce	Serves 4	470	18	11	1490	43	1	1	0	7
Cheesy Bean and Tomato Bake	Serves 4–6	330	13	4.5	1140	40	10	10	0	18
Stir-Fried Rice Cakes with Bok Choy and Snow Peas	Serves 4	440	15	7	870	73	2	42	37	7
Thai Red Curry with Bell Peppers and Tofu	Serves 4–6	260	21	13	340	12	1	5	2	10

Per Serving		Calories	Fat (g)	Saturated Fat (g)	Sodium (mg)	Carbohy-drates (g)	Fiber (g)	Total Sugar (g)	Added Sugar (g)	Protein (g)
CHAPTER 5 - SIDES										
Spice-Roasted Carrots	Serves 4	130	7	1	410	17	5	8	0	2
Honey Butter Corn	Serves 4	300	17	6	290	35	1	11	8	4
Sesame Green Beans	Serves 4	110	7	0.5	240	11	3	6	3	3
Watermelon and Cherry Tomato Salad	Serves 4	250	17	7	290	17	2	10	0	10
Garlic-Feta Cucumber Salad	Serves 4	140	14	3.5	280	3	1	1	0	3
Braised Red Potatoes	Serves 4–6	130	6	3.5	310	19	2	2	0	2
Lowcountry Red Rice	Serves 6	250	6	2	690	43	2	3	0	8
Brown Rice with Lime Dressing	Serves 4–6	250	11	1.5	50	38	3	3	3	3
Pearl Couscous with Herbs	Serves 4–6	210	4.5	0.5	200	36	0	1	0	6
Curried Chickpeas with Yogurt	Serves 6	170	9	1.5	450	16	5	1	0	6
Chickpeas with Garlic and Basil	Serves 6	160	9	1	450	15	5	1	0	6
Garlic Bread	Serves 8	260	13	7	460	29	0	2	0	5
Cheddar-Chive Biscuits	Per biscuit	270	18	11	320	21	0	2	1	6
CHAPTER 6 - SWEETS										
Chocolate Sugar Cookies	Per cookie	150	6	3.5	85	22	0	14	14	2
Cowboy Cookies	Per cookie	340	18	9	170	41	2	25	22	4
Brownie Bites	Per bite	80	4	0.5	30	12	0	9	9	1
Berry Streusel Bars	Per bar	150	6	4	45	22	0	12	6	1
Peanut Butter-Chocolate Tortilla Triangles	Serves 2	350	20	8	520	35	2	8	6	8
Coconut Snack Cake	Serves 12	210	10	8	190	26	0	15	11	3
Red Velvet Cupcakes	Per cupcake	260	13	9	170	30	0	21	20	3
Cream Cheese Frosting	Per 2 tablespoons	110	7	5	65	9	0	8	7	1
Skillet Stone Fruit Crisp	Serves 6	330	13	7	100	52	3	37	24	4
Lime Posset	Serves 6	380	29	18	25	31	1	29	22	3
Banana Cream Pie in a Jar	Serves 4	430	28	17	140	40	2	29	18	6
Whipped Cream	Per ¼ cup	110	11	7	10	2	0	2	2	1
Gajar Ka Halwa (Indian Carrot Pudding)	Serves 4	410	24	13	150	42	3	34	17	8

MEET OUR TEAM

Introducing America's Test Kitchen Kids!

This book was created by a group of passionate chefs, writers, editors, producers, educators, designers, and photographers. Our mission is to create a new generation of empowered cooks, engaged eaters, and curious experimenters.

MOLLY BIRNBAUM
Editor in Chief
I loved watching this whole book come together—from deciding which recipes to include, to the kitchen team testing them, to the editorial team writing content, to the photo and design teams creating a beautiful package. It's like teamwork magic!

SUZANNAH MCFERRAN
Executive Food Editor
I loved testing the Cucumber-Avocado Maki (page 88) at home with my daughter and her friends. Everyone was involved, and it was fun to see them realize just how easy it is to roll maki!

KRISTIN SARGIANIS
Executive Editor
I wish I had this book when I was a kid—I could have learned all these cooking techniques much sooner (and saved myself a lot of messes!). Don't sleep on the Creamy Secret Ingredient Pasta (page 96).

AFTON CYRUS
Deputy Food Editor
My favorite recipes that I developed for this book highlight core techniques that can serve kids in the kitchen for a lifetime, such as making perfectly cooked onions for Caramelized Onion Dip (page 62).

ANDREA RIVERA WAWRZYN
Associate Editor
I enjoy developing recipes that are hearty but also leave room for creativity, such as the Breakfast Quesadillas (page 38) and Kimchi-Miso Ramen (page 98).

KATY O'HARA
Associate Editor
Each chapter is full of delicious recipes, but I particularly enjoyed editing the dessert chapter. I've been dreaming about that Coconut Snack Cake (page 182).

TESS BERGER
Associate Editor
I loved taste-testing dozens of recipes in this book, but I have a soft spot for the Cheesy Bean and Tomato Bake (page 132). I couldn't get enough of all that saucy, crunchy, bean-y goodness!

ASHLEY STOYANOV
Photo Test Cook

I love cooking for family and friends, and the dinner chapter is full of awesome recipes for me to try on them, such as the Thai Red Curry with Bell Peppers and Tofu (page 136).

KRISTEN BANGO
Assistant Test Cook

My favorite recipe I worked on was definitely the Brownie Bites (page 172)! They reminded me of the Little Bites Fudge Brownies I grew up on, but 10 times better.

JULIA ARWINE
Editorial Assistant
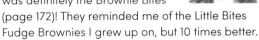
I loved trying new things. The first time I made Turkey and Cheddar Sandwiches with Pickled Apple (page 78), I liked them so much I had one every day for a week!

KEEHUP YONG
Senior Video Producer

I loved learning about proper cooking techniques while creating the videos for this, and I'm jealous of the young chefs who get to eat all these recipes!

KENZIE GRUENIG
Video Producer

There are so many cool tips and tricks packed into this book and the videos, and I'm excited for all the young chefs to up their game while watching them!

ANNY GUERZON
Assistant Video Editor
I loved collaborating with different members of the team to make the technique videos—being creative is way more fun with great company!

JACK BISHOP
Chief Creative Officer
The breakfast chapter has such creative recipes. I especially love the Breakfast Cookies (page 44). Who doesn't want to start the day with cookies?

LINDSEY TIMKO CHANDLER
Design Director

This book's photography puts a smile on my face. Planning the shoots was exciting, but it wasn't until we got into the photo studio that we discovered just how fun and beautiful the photography would turn out.

JANET TAYLOR
Deputy Art Director

I enjoyed designing this book with kids in mind by choosing vibrant colors, enticing photography, and showing recipe steps in a way that's easy to follow.

JULIE BOZZO COTE
Photography Director

My son and his friends participated in one of the photo shoots, and it was a blast to see them cook! I love the idea of kids working on cooking skills they can use forever!

MEREDITH MULCAHY
Senior Photo Producer
It was fun seeing how excited all of the families were to come into the photo studio—it encouraged me to cook more with my daughters.

KEVIN WHITE
Photographer
Photographing and tasting all the delicious food in this book was fun. I'm always amazed by this team's ability to make recipes full of flavor without being too complicated.

TRICIA NEUMYER
Production & Imaging Specialist

I love seeing everyone having fun creating great food. This book makes cooking empowering and inclusive, and inspires me to be more confident in the kitchen too!

INDEX